I'm Not a Mind Reader

Using the Power of Three-Dimensional Communication for a Better Relationship

Marty Babits

Health Communications, Inc.
Deerfield Beach, Florida

www.hcibooks.com

The vignettes in the book are based on true stories from my clients. I've changed the details to protect confidentiality.

Library of Congress Cataloging-in-Publication Data

Babits, Marty, 1948–
  I'm not a mind reader : using the power of three-dimensional communication for a better relationship / Marty Babits.
      pages cm
  Includes bibliographical references and index.
  ISBN-13: 978-0-7573-1833-7 (Paperback)
  ISBN-10: 0-7573-1833-9 (Paperback)
  ISBN-13: 978-0-7573-1834-4 (ePub)
  ISBN-10: 0-7573-1834-7 (e-Pub)
1. Communication in marriage.   2. Couples--Psychology.
3. Interpersonal communication.   4. Interpersonal relations.   I. Title.
  HQ734.B2117 2015
  302—dc23
                                                                    2015009083

Publisher: Health Communications, Inc.
          3201 S.W. 15th Street
          Deerfield Beach, FL 33442–8190

Cover design by Larissa Hise Henoch
Interior design and formatting by Lawna Patterson Oldfield

To Lisa, my beautiful wife

Contents

Part Three: Using Neuroscientific Breakthroughs for Better Relationships

Acknowledgments

I am lucky, grateful, and fortunate to have gotten the support I've had in writing this book.

Dan Smullyan demonstrated patience and grace in countless discussions of the writing at all stages. Thank you so much for that. Robert and Jane Nathanson read through the manuscript and gave me detailed feedback, which was enormously helpful. Shifra Levin did the same and made astute, useful comments. Thank you to Lew Frischman for your support and encouragement as well. Judith Friedman, thank you so much for the time and energy you put into helping me to clarify my thinking and writing. Allen Bergson read and commented on numerous sections of the writing and was a steady and steadying resource, as he has been for me for many years. Sister Trudy, Ken, Nicole, and Felicia Carter, as well, and sister Jane Babits and brother-in-law Toby Fagenson were supportive and encouraging when they were able to put down their guitars long enough to have a conversation. Toby, in particular, made a number of useful comments in the key of A natural. The guys from KV, the housing project on the lower east side of Manhattan where I grew up, fueled me with love, acceptance, and encouragement. We still get together and occasionally play punchball in Tanahe Park.

Many thanks go to Bob "Knucks" Nathanson, David "Ace" Bellel, Mark "Pudge" Schumer, and brother Stu, Murray "Rambo" Schefflin, Al "Long-Ball" Silverstein, and brother Howie, Lew "Rhythm King" Myer,

Richard "Energy King" Karney, Marv "Faster Than a Speeding Bullet" Kuperstein, and brother Jerry, Paul "Hoops" Levine, Kev "Newby" Baker, Bruce Bueller, and the inimitable Stewart Brokowsky, gone too soon. My son and talented thespian, Lucas, showed his own special brand of support. Matthew Devin, my nephew, a shout-out to you for your help.

I want to thank the Institute for Contemporary Psychotherapy (ICP), particularly the Family and Couples Treatment and Training Service, with special appreciation to Ella Lasky, Alison Kalfus, LouAnn Smith, Judi Price, Roberta Estar, Linda Bradley, Fran Hamburg, and Janet David.

I want to acknowledge the outstanding graduates I have had the privilege to work with over the past few years, among them Michael Nott, Johannes Wiedenmuller, Rachel Mann, Eva Kant, and too many others to name here.

I owe a debt of gratitude to my clients. I have learned more from you about three-dimensional communication than from any of the esteemed authorities, with the exception of D. W. Winnicott.

A thank-you to the Management Team at ICP, with special thanks to Ron Taffel and Rosemary Masters for help and support. Special thanks also to Elizabeth Danto, formerly Division Director at Hunter Graduate School of Social Work; your encouragement and support have been important to me.

I'm grateful for my editor, Christine Belleris, whose advice and opinions have been helpful and steadying. I want to thank my agent, Nancy Rosenfeld, for her loyalty and support. I also would like to thank Kim Weiss, Ian Briggs, and the entire HCI family for believing in this project.

A thank-you to Uncle Joe Borrucker for your enduring and heroic spirit; to Marisa, Bill, Jolyn, Emil, and Gloria; to Linda Babits and Laura Martin; to Mary Jane, Tom, Nora, Liam, and Julia; and also Theresa, Jayson, Rio Lee Weingast, Sean K., Corny and Brendan, Ed and Sam. I know I've missed some important names, please forgive me.

I saved the sweetest for the closing, the dessert principle, if you will. The heart of my heart, Lisa, my beautiful wife, thank you for your support, intelligent and grounded feedback, and, most of all, love.

Introduction

The first duty of love is to listen.
—Paul Tillich

Interested in Improving Communication?

If you are interested in improving communication in your relationship, *I'm Not a Mind Reader* is for you. Many couples cite poor communication as the biggest obstacle to feeling close. Most of them have a hard time envisioning how it can be improved.

- ♥ They do not understand that communication between partners has an inherent structure.
- ♥ They confuse the various dimensions of communication.
- ♥ They argue in such a way that damages trust.
- ♥ They allow resentment to shut down their dialogue.
- ♥ They allow blame and self-righteousness to obscure possibilities for resolving issues effectively.

There is an antidote to this constellation of toxic communication problems: three-dimensional communication. I will teach you what it is and how to use it effectively. Like the majority of the couples I see in my office, if you need help fixing your communication process, this book will help you.

Communication Versus Dysfunctional Talk

The word *communication* is derived from the Latin word *communicare*, which means "sharing." When true to its roots, communication brings people together. Dysfunctional attempts to communicate do not achieve this end. Good communication, *three-dimensional communication*, creates emotional safety.

You may have questions about what emotional safety is, how it works, how it can be created, and how it is connected to each dimension of communication. Chapter Two, "Emotional Safety," answers these and many other questions. For now, the short answer is that good communication rests on maintaining a continuous awareness of opportunities for creating emotional safety.

Three-dimensional communication *generates* emotional safety. As a mindful practice, it will change the way you think about what communication itself is.

A Positive Mind-Set

A positive mind-set alone cannot guarantee improved understanding between you and your partner. If your mind-set is not positive, failure is guaranteed.

You may be wondering what constitutes a positive mind-set. As represented in the work of psychologist Dr. Carol Dweick and stated briefly, it is a *learning* mind-set; a mind-set that becomes energized by challenge. The opposite, what Dweick calls a *fixed* mind-set, retreats from challenge, avoids it.

Despite intelligence and competence at acquiring rote information, people with a fixed mind-set are ill-prepared to go beyond where they have been. Yet the life cycle invariably confronts all of us with new difficulties. Accordingly, we need a learning mind-set; it is not a developmental frill. It is a developmental necessity.

Three-Dimensional Communication

Every message from one partner to another can be considered in terms of three separate dimensions. The first is the surface level. This refers to the *literal meaning* of what partners say to each other. The second is the emotional subtext of the message, its emotional undertone or undercurrent. The third dimension involves evaluating the first two and comparing that combination with the goal of creating emotional safety within the dialogue.

With all three dimensions active and coordinated, communication provides a sense of direction for the dialogue because this question is addressed: Are you going toward or away from building emotional safety? This method strengthens your ability to appreciate the potential, in whatever situation you are in, for moving toward creating emotional safety.

The First Dimension

In a nutshell, difficulties that occur in the first dimension are simple misunderstandings. Incomplete messages and misheard or misspoken phrases: that is the stuff of first-dimension breakdowns in communication.

Part of what has to happen in an intimate long-term relationship is for partners to get to know themselves and each other better and better over time. Few relationships start out with a solid foundation of effective communication. Most of us have a lot of learning and growing to do before we are even close to being as loving and humane as we can be. The place where this learning can be accomplished? In your relationship.

Carole and Jim had arranged to meet on 96th Street. They frequently met on that large thoroughfare; however, neither had specified the corner they would be waiting on. They often met at the corner closest to the park, 96th and West End Avenue, which is where Jim waited expectantly. Carole recalled instantly when they had made the arrangement that the very last time they'd met on 96th Street, it was at 96th and Amsterdam. As a result, they did not find each other. Each felt self-righteous about having done the right thing, and each was convinced that the other had made a mistake. Although this situation sounds like a caricature of miscommunication, it is based on a real occurrence. It can also be read as a metaphor for how partners often fail to spell out information adequately for each other. And how, despite the incompleteness of their messages to each other, they often expect that their partner should have understood *what had never been said*. This is a miscommunication in the first dimension. The literal messages were inadequate to foster a secure understanding.

> **Jim:** Can you meet me at 96th Street?
> **Carole:** When?
> **Jim:** Five thirty in the afternoon. Tomorrow.
> **Carole:** Okay. See you then.

Neither intuited that the omitted detail would be important. They both believed they knew what the other meant.

The Second Dimension

As mentioned above, in the second dimension we focus on grasping aspects of the message that lie underneath the words, the subtext. Tone of voice, gesture—verbal, facial, postural (body language)—all of these affect the meaning that is embedded within the words themselves. The emotional subtext or undercurrent of the message makes up the second dimension.

For example, the phrase *I'm glad you're here* spoken with a loving tone can strengthen a feeling of connection. The same phrase delivered with a sarcastic tone or a roll of the eyes reverses the meaning. This creates distance. The tone of any message, heart of the second dimension, is critical to the meaning of the message conveyed.

Often the first and second dimensions appear to conflict with each other. This becomes the mixed message that we all are probably familiar with as a concept and, regrettably, as an experience. A mixed message is when the tone or implication of a statement contradicts the words. John says, "I'm sorry to hear that you didn't get the job," and smirks—a classic mixed message.

Last but Far from Least, the Third Dimension

The third dimension opens the door to possibilities for deepest connection. It gives a couple's communication richness and depth.

In the third dimension you monitor whether the communication process you are participating in brings you and your partner closer together or not. This dimension connects you to your reflective capacity. This third dimension lights up a circuit that includes your capacities to compare and contrast what you are thinking about the dialogue of the moment and your long-range goals and objectives for your relationship. It brings you into greater contact with the fullness of your cognitive, emotional, and decision-making abilities. In this sense the third dimension is your portal to mindfulness.

Not every pair establishes a third dimension in their process. Listen to a snippet of Kelly and Joe's conversation:

> **Kelly:** Please don't purchase the new computer until a week after we've deposited our paychecks and paid the bills.
>
> **Joe:** Don't you have anything better to do than police my spending habits?
>
> **Kelly:** We spoke about this and agreed to hold off until we were in a better position, savings-wise, to make discretionary purchases.

Joe: You take the spontaneity out of our relationship.

Kelly: And you take the common sense out of having a conversation. Would you grow up!

The aftermath of this exchange was a breakdown in conversation. The talk escalated into a yelling match followed by tears and then a wary standoff. Talks like these damage trust. The interaction illustrates the lack of three-dimensional depth in Kelly and Joe's communication at the time of the talk.

What if Joe had responded to Kelly this way:

Kelly: Please don't purchase the new computer until a week after we've deposited our paychecks and paid the bills.

Joe: You'd like it if I waited before I buy the new computer. I hear you, but I really don't want to wait.

Kelly: We spoke about this and agreed to hold off until we were in a better position, savings-wise, to make discretionary purchases.

Joe: I'm excited about getting it as soon as possible. And I need it for my work. I did agree to hold off, but it's hard to do. What about if I wait until next Friday, a week from today? Most of the bills will be paid by then. Can we agree about that?

Kelly: How about if we agree to talk about it on Friday and see where we are then. I'd love for you to get what you need. I'm just worried about staying on budget. We've both talked about how important that is right now.

Joe: Fair enough. We'll talk about it then.

In this second version of the conversation, Kelly's thoughts and feelings are not discounted and neither are Joe's. Regardless of how the issue is resolved, the difference between the two conversations is significant. In the second version, a dialogue has commenced, but it was not short-circuited because a difference was expressed. This is important. Joe has demonstrated that he is including Kelly's thoughts and feelings in his own thinking. She does not feel attacked or minimized as she had in the first version of the talk. In the second version, Joe takes Kelly's perspective seriously. As a result, she responds to him sympathetically. They are allies in conversation, not adversaries in an argument. Version one of the talk is a road map to separation; version two, a blueprint for working through problems.

In the pages to come, the couples and issues you'll read about will likely sound familiar. They are presented to illustrate how improvements in communication became possible for them. They can become possible for you as well. Of course, names have been changed to protect privacy.

The Making of a Couples Therapist

Many years ago, before I knew I would become a therapist, I sat in an office talking about couples' communication issues. The discussion came around to ways in which partners can monitor their individual feelings and what makes this so important in relationships. I was one of the two clients. I learned a lot that day. It was my first exposure to couples work.

I realized then that I had never witnessed the couple I knew best up to that point in my life—my parents—talking through difficulties. For that matter, strong as their relationship was in some ways, I was unaware of whether they had ever been able to work through differences. I was aware of many arguments but not of any that either got resolved or turned into discussions in which either my mother or father considered the other's perspective in a calm manner. This possibility of thoughtful discussion lay outside of my personal experience. I had never witnessed it firsthand.

For better or worse, my parents vented at each other periodically but, as far as I could tell, had no ambition to *resolve* problems. Given these experiences, I guess it's not surprising that the idea that problems between partners could be resolved was something of a revelation to me.

During the couple sessions, I learned things about how I interacted with my partner. I also became aware that I had blind spots, areas I didn't understand about myself and also areas I wasn't aware I was confused about. For example, I took for granted that I knew what my partner would or wouldn't like, based on general assumptions that might be true much of the time but incorrect some of the time. I did not think to include her in some of the social occasions I attended, thinking she would feel relieved not to be asked. I hadn't been aware that I did that. I also hadn't been aware that I was causing her to feel excluded when I made these kinds of assumptions. I came to see other ways in which I had misunderstood and needed to improve my ways of interacting with my partner. The two-part big takeaway: I needed to know myself better than I did, and attaining this self-awareness was possible, for the process had already begun.

Familiarity may breed contempt for some in certain circumstances. But it lays the foundation for intimacy for most of us. To appreciate feeling loved, we must feel known and understood. A deep and intimate familiarity between partners is the hallmark of a three-dimensional connection. The therapist back then helped me see what my expectations were for my relationship. She helped me explore the feelings and attitudes that lay embedded within my expectations. My experience with this therapist influenced me in becoming a couples therapist myself.

Acknowledge Feelings;
Don't Be Controlled by Them

Many partners despair about possibilities for change. To the extent that you feel despair about changing your relationship for the better, it's important that you acknowledge you feel this way. But, at the same time, acknowledge that this is a *feeling*, not an irreversible and situation-defining fact. Many times you will be able to work through this feeling to reach an outcome that exceeds your expectations. You owe it to yourself and your relationship to work with this reality in mind.

Learning that we can cope with stress energizes us. Also, the stress of life reinforces a message that we cannot afford to ignore: Being able to rely on ourselves *and* those we are close to is our greatest stress-reducing strategy. We each encounter moments of great stress, and at those times, feeling we are alone can terrify and potentially paralyze us. Feeling supported makes all the difference. We become more optimistic, and that optimism helps us approach whatever problem we need to solve with greater focus and inventiveness.

Unique Qualities of Emotional Safety

I talk a lot about emotional safety throughout this book. What follows is an anecdote that will give you the flavor of the concept the way I'm using it:

I went to my eye doctor because my right eye felt itchy. The problem probably would have gone away by itself, but I figured I was due for a checkup and it wouldn't hurt to get some input from a professional as to what was going on.

The doctor said that because I had worn contact lenses for many years, I might have developed a common condition: dry eye syndrome. Dr. Destin said, "Should it turn out that you have this problem,

I have good news for you. There are eye drops, free of side effects, that remedy it in a very special way. The drops create an atmosphere within the eye that brings the eye's natural ability to regulate itself back to full functionality. They do not so much cure the eye as prepare the eye to cure itself."

Emotional safety works in relationships in a way that parallels this process. The drops create an environment within the core of the eye that promotes resilience and healthful self-regulation. That's what emotional safety does within your relationship. If difficulties set in without emotional safety there is a downward spiral. With emotional safety, problems can be acknowledged and overcome. This makes it good medicine.

Take a minute to think about this point: Whether we are talking about emotional safety or the eye drops, the "cure" does not make the situation better by *attacking* the problem. Both remedies set up the conditions under which healthy rebalancing can take place.

How can I teach you to prepare and make effective use of my prescription? How and why does creating emotional safety improve things so dramatically?

KEY POINT: sometimes we try to get rid of a problem by doing what we can to destroy it. In other words, we give our full attention and energy to the negative that is plaguing us and set out to eliminate it. Chemotherapy is a good example of this strategy for cure. Another good example in the inter-personal realm would be partners who war with each other in the hopes of overcoming their disappointments and dissatisfactions. They attempt to obliterate the part of their partner with which they are disappointed. It never works. This strategy is self-defeating because it does not bring about the conditions that sustain love and trust. In fact, couples who primarily rail at each other, complaining and blaming, do not rid themselves of the problems they are complaining about. They make them worse or cause separation. By creating three-dimensional communication and an atmosphere of emotional safety, we set the stage for a healthy, more positive environment in which the relationship can rebalance and the partners can move toward better self-regulation.

♥ ♥ ♥

Old scripts get replayed over and over in relationships that are stuck. And the old scripts are stale to begin with. Partners need new scripts. Some books provide actual scripts. That is fine and can be helpful. I will give examples of new ways you can talk and behave with your partner. Good scripts provide advantages. But it's the attitude—the mind-set—that underlies the words that is even more crucial. And what makes all the difference is whether the lines of the script are supported by an emotional undercurrent of acceptance and warmth, as opposed to an undercurrent of contempt or impatience. Are the first and second dimensions of communication in sync with each other? If not, attempts at making contact turn into a game of push-pull. And does the script connect to the third dimension? Tracking the complexity of three-dimensional communication becomes second nature when you practice it regularly. Getting positive results through practice makes it easier to continue to get positive results. Breakthroughs create breakthroughs.

What Never Works?

Partners who try to force their partners to change are categorically unsuccessful. It never works. This strategy does not bring about the conditions that sustain love and trust. By creating three-dimensional communication and an atmosphere of emotional safety, we set the stage for a healthy environment in which the relationship can rebalance and in which partners can move toward better self-regulation.

How Is This Book Organized?

Part One of Three is comprised of Chapters One through Four.

In this first part, I introduce a foundation for understanding, think-ing about, and working with the structure of couples communication. Many of us are not clear as to what it means to say that communica-tion has a structure. I prepare you to customize the ideas presented here so you can apply them to your own situation. Following this Introduction you'll find a three-dimensionality exercise, which will help you gauge the extent to which you currently have (or do not have) a three-dimensional communication pattern in your life. After finishing the book, I recommend that you retake this quiz. I predict that the before and after comparison will be useful and gratifying.

In Chapter One I describe the elements that will prepare you for the changes that lie ahead, and the three dimensions of communica-tion are discussed more fully. In Chapter Two, emotional safety is the topic. In this chapter, and peppered throughout the book, you'll find exercises and questionnaires to help you integrate three-dimensional communication concepts and skills.

I highlight particular ways in which Carole and Jim, a couple I worked with for some time, progressed from bitterness to a three-dimensional connection in Chapter Four. They learned to de-escalate anger by resolving it, not merely side-stepping it. As they bring emo-tional safety into their communication pattern, compassion develops too. *Willingness* is a grossly underdiscussed and undervalued aspect of communication. It is the main subject of the chapter. The desire to change from having a pattern of expressing anger destructively to one in which you and your partner express anger mindfully requires willingness and perseverance.

In Part Two we will turn our attention to a second couple, Diane and Jaime. We analyze the factors that prevented them from being able to resolve their problems peaceably without having to separate first. We also come to terms with how and why their initial responses to feeling misunderstood by each other prevented them from building a three-dimensional communication process. How do they recover their relationship? That's the heart of this section of the book.

In Part Three, the final section of the book, we explore ways of using recent neuroscientific breakthroughs to help make good decisions about how and when to raise difficult issues.

On the next page you can assess the levels of three-dimensionality and emotional safety in your relationship. Directions for self-scoring and interpretation of results are included.

EXERCISE

Your Three-Dimensionality Quotient

How grounded is your communication with your partner? Is your communication three-dimensional? Emotionally safe? Find out.

Circle the number from 1 to 4, depending on how accurately or inaccurately it describes what goes on between you and your partner. (Male and female pronouns alternate for reliability only.)

1 = Never; **2** = Not Usually; **0** = Neutral or Not Applicable; **3** = Usually; **4** = Always

1) When my partner and I disagree about something, it escalates into a conversation that causes hurt feelings.

| 1 | 2 | 0 | 3 | 4 |

2) Given the way I communicate with my partner at present, I would expect that he would take my opinions and ideas seriously, whether or not he agrees with me.

| 1 | 2 | 0 | 3 | 4 |

3) I do not appreciate my partner asking questions about how I feel. If she has to ask questions, it already feels like I'm alone with what I am going through.

| 1 | 2 | 0 | 3 | 4 |

4) When there is an awareness that either my own or my partner's feelings have been hurt, we tend to quickly resolve the issue that caused the hurt. In the end, we consider the issue resolved when we both feel that our feelings have been understood, acknowledged, and appreciated by the other.

| 1 | 2 | 0 | 3 | 4 |

5) My partner feels that I ask questions about his feelings in order to use the information against him.

1   2   0   3   4

6) My partner and I speak candidly about ways in which we enjoy being with each other sexually.

1   2   0   3   4

7) I feel helpless to get my partner to focus on and take in my point of view.

1   2   0   3   4

8) When it comes to money issues, my partner and I are able to help each other think through and express differences in a calm and respectful manner.

1   2   0   3   4

9) I expect my partner to satisfy my social needs.

1   2   0   3   4

10) My partner makes an effort to find out how I feel.

1   2   0   3   4

11) My partner and I go to bed angry.

1   2   0   3   4

12) I may know a lot about myself but, at the same time, I learn new things about myself all the time.

1   2   0   3   4

13) I find myself thinking, "People who have trouble making decisions annoy me."

1   2   0   3   4

14) I am curious about and interested in how my partner feels, and I believe that she understands that well.

    1   2   0   3   4

15) My partner gives me the "cold shoulder."

    1   2   0   3   4

16) Decision making with my partner is open and collaborative.

    1   2   0   3   4

17) I crave acknowledgment from my partner that he is responsible for the problems in our relationship.

    1   2   0   3   4

18) I feel included in small decisions, such as what we eat for dinner.

    1   2   0   3   4

19) When my opinion is very different from my partner's, she ridicules me.

    1   2   0   3   4

20) When I am upset it is a comfort to speak with my partner.

    1   2   0   3   4

21) My partner rolls his eyes at me when I speak.

    1   2   0   3   4

22) My partner confers with me before changing plans that we have agreed upon together

    1   2   0   3   4

23) I find myself thinking, "I believe that my partner would treat me better if she truly loved me."

    1   2   0   3   4

24) My partner is important to me, but my friends are also very important to me.

1   2   0   3   4

♥ ♥ ♥

Scoring Instructions:

Add all the scores of the odd-numbered items: (1, 3, 5, 7 . . . 23)
Odd-numbered total: _____

Add all the scores from the even-numbered items: (2, 4, 6, 8 . . . 24)
Even-numbered total: _____

If the odd-numbered total is greater than the even-numbered total, subtract the greater from the lesser number and then follow the number with a hyphen and the word *Odd*.

For example, if the odd-numbered total is larger than the even-numbered total by 20, the final score is 20-Odd.

If the even-numbered total is greater than the odd-numbered total, subtract the greater from the lesser number and then follow the number with a hyphen and the word *Even*.

For example, if the even-numbered total is larger than the odd-numbered total by 20, the final score is 20-Even.

Final Score: _____ – _____ *(Odd or Even, depending on which total was larger)*

Results Analysis:

33-Even to 27-Even: You have a strong head start in both building emotional safety and communicating three-dimensionally. There is evidence of much empathy, caring, and love in your relationship.

26-Even to 22-Even: You have significant strengths in your relationship. Work on slowing down the communication process so that you build understanding not only on what you think your partner has said or done but on what he intended to say or do. Effort to understand whether this discrepancy—between what you think your partner means to say and what he intends—will move your dialogue forward. You have good reason to feel hopeful about making progress by deepening emotional safety and three-dimensional communication with your partner.

21-Even to 0: You have strengths in your relationship but also many points of confusion and disconnection. Please go over examples of three-dimensional communication and all the exercises in this book carefully. Your potential to make great progress with your partner is within reach but will take perseverance.

33-Odd to 27-Odd: You and your partner rarely see eye to eye. Perhaps you need to speak to each other about whether you are willing to try to make things better with each other. If you can get a commitment to work on problems together, the relationship can advance toward the realm of empathy and trust quickly. If not, the situation seems extremely difficult—not hopeless but difficult. Before giving up or deciding that things are too hard to change, attempt to make the ideas connected to three-dimensional communication and emotional safety come alive for you. You probably feel alone much of the time, even when you are with your partner. Keep in mind that he or she likely feels the same way too. If you can establish a common goal—helping each other feel better when you are together—it can go a long way toward changing the mood of the relationship for the better. If your score is in this range, I invite you, after working with the ideas in this book, to write me and let me know if *I'm Not a Mind Reader* has been helpful to you. I promise to respond to your e-mail.

26-Odd to 22-Odd: A formidable amount of conflict and attitudes have hardened so that it is likely you and your partner feel like adversaries as often (or more often) as you feel like allies. Despite the problems, concerted effort at learning to build emotional safety and three-dimensional communication can help you make changes that you may now feel are beyond your capability. Do not give up without trying to improve things, but be wary of overextending yourself. You will not be able to improve the relationship on your own. You will need your partner's active support and cooperation.

21-Odd to 1-Odd: Your relationship is fraught with disappointment and loneliness. You show signs of wanting to break out of the confusion. Persevere and you will be able to assess your relationship's true potential for improved communication and loving goodwill.

Part One

A Foundation for Understanding

CHAPTER ONE

Exploring Three Dimensions

The capacity for hope is the most significant fact of life. It provides human beings with a sense of destination and the energy to get started.

—Norman Cousins

The experiences of Carole and Jim, a couple I worked with in my private practice, are a good vehicle for illustrating how three-dimensional communication can become integrated into a couple's way of communicating. (To protect confidentiality, names and some details have been changed.)

Knowledge of the three dimensions enables you to identify opportunities for connection. Some of these would otherwise be invisible, unrecognizable, even unfathomable prior to knowing what you were looking to find. That's partly because you will learn not only how to look for these opportunities but how to create them.

Meet Carole and Jim

Carole, Jim's wife, felt so unnerved by a conversation they'd had that the very next day she called to make an appointment for couples work. The message she left on my answering machine said that she and her husband "needed help communicating."

One week later, I met Carole and Jim for the first time. With her black hair pulled back into a French twist, Carole carried grace and determination in every step from waiting room to consulting room.

Once she was seated, her bearing changed from the composed and resolute woman I'd first seen to that of a crumpled and sad-eyed rag doll. Without saying a word, tears formed at the corners of her eyes and ran down her cheeks. She stared straight down at the carpet before her. Carole had been in individual therapy at the time of her parents' divorce, when she was seventeen years old, but had never been in couples therapy before.

Jim spoke first. Layered into his thick New York accent was a subtle brogue that evinced his childhood in Donegal, northwestern Ireland. Jim's gray-blue eyes darted from side to side. I surmised that the office felt strange to him. When he told me that he had never been to a therapist before, I wasn't surprised. He had the look of someone who didn't know what to expect next.

Jim began. "We're here because we don't seem to be able to talk to each other without fighting." He paused. "And when we don't talk, it gets worse."

Carole countered. "He can talk the talk and make you think he's interested in working things out. But he doesn't follow through. When it comes to making the talk count, I feel like I've been on my own a long time now." The sadness in her face had disappeared, and the look of determination returned. "He speaks up when he doesn't like what I say but otherwise won't participate in conversation. I don't know how to reach him." She paused. "It frightens me." Her tears streamed again.

Then Jim's eyes grew moist and overflowed as well. It became a moment of silence infused with tenderness.

After the quiet I asked Jim, "How does it feel to hear your partner say that she is frightened and doesn't feel she knows how to reach you? Does that surprise you?"

The lilt in his reply gave his words an ironic twist. "No. I'm used to that kind of thing. It might surprise me if I *didn't* hear it."

Carole rolled her eyes and then looked down at the carpet again. Her facial expression hardened.

I wondered what had become of the brief moment of shared tears. Was this how they dealt with moments of contact? By repudiating them? By reinstating a casual sarcasm? By undermining whatever understanding they may have reached?

The First Dimension

The first dimension of Carole and Jim's communication—or anyone's—is its literal meaning. Think of the script of a play—the words as written would be the first dimension of the conversation. Those words, that dialogue, its surface meaning, plain and simple.

Jim: We're here because we don't seem to be able to talk to each other without fighting. And when we don't talk, it gets worse.

Carole: He speaks up when he doesn't like what I say but otherwise won't talk much. I don't know how to reach him.

In terms of this interchange, in the first dimension Jim has made a statement, and Carole's response ignores its content; it shows no sign of Carole having received his message. They are missing each other. There is no connection between the two statements. In this sense, the interchange is dysfunctional. The first dimension, when it is effective, helps partners locate each other "on the same page" of their dialogue.

Clearly Jim and Carole are not on the same page. At this point they may not even be working with the same book!

When people misspeak, mishear, misunderstand, confuse, conflate, or otherwise misconstrue what has been said, errors at this level are serious and can lead to problems. If and when lapses in the first dimension of communication occur and can be understood as miscommunication, resentment can sometimes be repaired quickly. To clarify further: When considering the first dimension, we are talking about the messages passed back and forth without regard to implication, innuendo, or personalized interpretation of any sort. Those qualities constitute the second dimension of communication (the emotional subtext). When a partner's first dimensional message gets lost, as Jim's does here, the lack of connection, even on a superficial level, is significant. The simplest "way back" from this sort of disconnection is the offer of acknowledgment/appreciation for what has been said. This conveys an acceptance of the importance of the other's participation in the dialogue.

Misunderstandings create distance and distrust. Still, research indicates that neither the intensity nor the frequency of arguments around misunderstandings indicates a problematic relationship. What is most crucial is whether the misunderstandings get resolved and whether partners make attempts to revisit and repair hurts. If partners have a satisfactory communication process that allows them to resolve misunderstandings effectively, that is to say, to avoid holding on to grudges, the superficial fireworks of arguments, even frequent arguments, are decidedly secondary, even unimportant. What separates a functional communication style from a broken-down pattern is the ability to make repairs. The couple that clarifies differences and moves on to reconnection, that does not get preoccupied with establishing who was right and who was wrong about the misunderstanding, has a lot going for them. Right and wrong starts out and remains a secondary concern. In this way arguments do not rupture trust.

Did They Say What They Meant to Say?

Partners sometimes need help articulating their ideas clearly. Before countering your partner for what you believe he or she meant to say, it sometimes helps immensely if you clarify whether your understanding of what was said matches what he or she intended to convey. Slowing down the dialogue between you and your partner to include a step like this brings mindfulness to your process. If this is a regular part of your communication process, it gives you a chance to examine your partner's message and provides opportunities for you to help each other clarify not only what is said but, even more important, what needs to be said.

This outlook brings flexibility and a collaborative spirit into your dialogue. It often is the case that what is going on beyond the words that are spoken is the major issue—the feelings underneath the words, the motivation for the words, and the implications of the words. For that we move on to discussion of the second dimension.

The Second Dimension

The second dimension of communication is made up of the emotional undertone of any message. Tone of voice, turn of phrase, subtle gestures, whether verbal, facial, or postural (body language), all of these can affect the meaning that is embedded within the message. Not only the power and scope but the understandability of many messages depends on the second dimension.

Attitudes such as graciousness, warmth, contempt, impatience, as well as expectations of being understood or misunderstood, and all other attitudes that color communication comprise the second dimension. Using words or nonverbal cues, the speaker can signal that she is positioning herself above, below, or on the same level as the listener—another key aspect of the second dimension.

When we think of a statement that prompts this response, "I heard the words she spoke, but I believe what she *really* meant was something very different," we are intimating—as is sometimes the case—that the second dimension tells a different and more fundamental story than the words by themselves do.

The Third Dimension

Visualize two partners using a makeshift setup to get their messages across to each other. The setup resembles a primitive phone connection with two receiver instruments into which they can speak and listen. A sheathed cable that looks like a telephone line with three wires bundled within join the receivers. Each of the three wires represents one of the dimensions of communication.

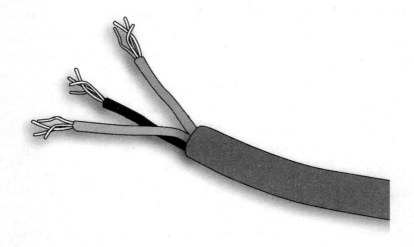

The third wire of the communication cable is the ground. We have reviewed what the first and second dimensions involve. It is by using this third dimension that partners activate their reflective capacity. This allows them to consider the meaning of dimensions one and two. When this third pathway is active and functional, partners are able to absorb the second dimension of the message—the emotional undertone—and bring that together with the literal meaning spoken. Within the third dimension, the first and second are compared and contrasted with the goals of the relationship.

By goals of the relationship, I include the specific hopes and dreams of the partners. And also I include something else many partners are not able to envision with clarity: the goal of creating emotional safety.

In the third dimension:

- ❤ Partners judge whether their conversation adds to or detracts from an atmosphere of *emotional safety* in the relationship.
- ❤ Without emotional safety, partners navigate their relationship blind, or, as Daniel Siegel writes, they relate to each other *mindblind*. This means that they are oblivious to each other's internal realities. They do not have a sense of what is going on within each other. Among other things, this makes empathy impossible.
- ❤ They may hear the words (first dimension) each other says but be oblivious to understanding the emotional, spiritual, or even cognitive matrix from which the remark emerges.
- ❤ To have a meeting of the minds, couples must connect on all three dimensions. The meeting of minds involves more than the hearing of words.

I've described what happens when the third dimension is not functioning.

What does an activated third dimension do for a couple?

♥ Mitigates stress.

♥ Tones down anger.

♥ Absorbs anxiety.

♥ Prevents small mishaps from causing disproportionate rup-
tures in trust. It keeps small problems in perspective.

The third dimension grounds interpersonal communication the
way the ground in an electrical wire protects transmissions from
causing circuits to short out or overheat. Wouldn't that be a great
feature to have within a communication system? A mechanism
that prevents shorts and overheating, so that neural networks run
smoothly and hum along in harmony within each individual and
two-person system. Providing just that ground is a key attribute of
three-dimensional communication!

Without the third dimension, partners face one of two difficult
situations. Either they are in a state of hypervigilance because any
rupture in connection looms as a threat to the core of the relationship, or they become inured to the threat of danger and a mood of
recklessness emerges—a "What's the difference?" attitude.

♥ ♥ ♥

Does this way of thinking about communication represent a significant change from the way you have been thinking about what
good communication is?

Love alone is not enough to produce emotional safety. But if love
is there, it can help you to gather other needed resources along the
way to creating emotional safety.

If either you or your partner develops awareness of the lack of a
safe ground in your dialogue, please consider taking a step toward
developing one because the potential to develop this third dimension
hinges on awareness of the need for it!

MINI-EXERCISE: Jot down the concept of good communication that you have held prior to reading about three-dimensional communication. Either at this point or as you discover more about three-dimensional communication, compare and contrast the ideas you had embraced with those presented here. How is three-dimensional communication the same as or different from your original thoughts on how communication in your relationship needs to be developed?

EXERCISE 1.1

Practice in Bringing the Three Dimensions of Communication into Focus

Practice analyzing these short conversations in terms of the three dimensions of communication. You can check your responses against mine in Appendix 6. This is not a test or an exercise in correctness versus incorrectness. It is designed to provide practice in using the concepts involved in three-dimensional communication and to help you gain confidence in your ability to understand the structure of a conversation.

> **George:** I can't go on like this. You seem to think that all you have to do is nod your head and your part in the communication process is over. There's more to it, and I'm feeling beaten down by what you're doing.
>
> **Marie:** Isn't it the woman who's supposed to be famous for exaggerating and getting overly emotional about things? Get a grip on yourself.

Describe George and Marie's communication process based on this snippet of their conversation.

First Dimension: _____

_____

Second Dimension: _____

_____

Third Dimension: _____

_____

> **Valerie:** I want to see if we can figure out how we are going to handle the insurance payments along with the rest of our budget.
>
> **Charlotte:** I'd love to help you, but you know this is not my strong point.

Valerie: Well, it may not be your strong point, but if we could do this together, I'd feel good about it. In the end, your money is going into the plan with mine, and I'd like to know that you feel you had input. I'm not comfortable managing both of our monies.

Charlotte: Okay. That makes sense. Only I do trust you.

Valerie: I'm glad to hear that because there have been times in the past when I've spent our funds and you got angry because you didn't agree with how I allocated the money. Then I felt I should have made more of an effort to include you, but it was already too late.

Charlotte: That makes sense. What if I promise not to complain?

Valerie: Honestly, it's not just the possibility of a complaint; it's also that you might have a perspective on certain things that helps me figure out what I want and what would be best for us. I'd like it if we could do this together. It doesn't have to be fifty-fifty input all the way down the line, but it puts a lot of responsibility on me to make all the decisions and have all the information. I'd appreciate it if you play a more active role in this.

Charlotte: Okay. I'm going to try to participate more than I do with money decisions. I'm good with that.

First Dimension: _____

_____

Second Dimension: _____

_____

Third Dimension: _____

_____

Courtney: I never thought I'd make it through that dinner without either screaming or crying.

Chris: I know what you mean. My parents kept going on and on about the problem they've been having with their neighbor, and it was hard to make any contact with them on any other subject.

Courtney: Thank you for noticing. I thought I was going crazy there.

Chris: I feel the same way with them often. For some reason, I wasn't bothered as much tonight, but I can understand what you are talking about.

Courtney: That makes me feel better.

Chris: I'm glad. We made it through. I think that, in spite of their preoccupations, they appreciated our visit. It means a lot to me that you were able to join me today.

First Dimension: _____

_____

Second Dimension: _____

_____

Third Dimension: _____

_____

Think of a recent conversation you had with your partner. Try to think of one that involved a conflict or misunderstanding. Jot it down as fully as possible and then analyze it into the three dimensions.

First Dimension: _____

_____

Second Dimension: _____

_____

Third Dimension: _____

_____

Strengths: _____

Weaknesses: _____

Intentionality: _____

Validation: _____

Appreciation: _____

Acknowledgment: _____

Affirmation: _____

EXERCISE 1.2

More Practice Working
with the Three Dimensions of
Couples Communication

Alana found that after three drinks, her partner, Ken, was difficult to be around. He tended to become argumentative and was quick to pass judgment on her and anyone else around. They were planning to visit Alana's family when Ken mentioned that he was looking forward to having a few drinks and relaxing once they got there.

Alana said, "I am feeling exhausted and starting to get a headache. Would you mind driving us home after the visit?"

"Sure, no problem," Ken responded without hesitation.

"I really appreciate your doing that, Ken. I don't want to put a cramp in your evening, but I really don't think I'll be up to the driving later tonight."

"No problem. I don't feel like it will cramp my evening. I'm looking forward to having a relaxing time," Ken said.

"That's great. It makes me feel good to hear that you are looking forward to having a good time, even if you won't be drinking."

Ken's face turned red. "What are you talking about? Why are you always trying to control me? My drinking is my business, and I don't appreciate your getting in the middle of it."

"That doesn't make sense, Ken. I just asked you if you would drive us home. Are you going to drink and drive?"

"I can handle a few drinks and drive back with no problem. I said I'd drive and I'll be fine to drive. But I'll do it my own way."

How would you analyze this conversation?

Note below any problems you see in the first dimension of communication.

What do you think the most significant aspect of the second dimension of communication is in this conversation?

How about the third dimension of either Alana's and Ken's communication process?

After you have worked out your own response, turn to Appendix 6 for a discussion of my analysis of the conversation.

Conversational Interlude 1

I Can't Read Your Mind
What's not happening here?

Olivia: If you really loved me, you'd know what I need and I wouldn't have to tell you.

Norton: I do love you, and please tell me what you need so that I can show it.

Olivia: That shouldn't be necessary.

Norton: You're right.

Olivia: Really. Do you think so?

Norton: Absolutely. It shouldn't be this difficult for us to communicate. And you should know that I love you without my having to remind you about it time and time again by jumping through hoops.

Olivia: Oh, so I should know you love me without your having to remind me? So you have no responsibility to spell it out for me? I should just read your mind? That is so disappointing to hear.

Norton: Well, I was disappointed too. You're telling me. It hurts to have to say so.

Olivia: Hurts you?

Norton: Of course, but it's nice of you to talk about it. I didn't think you were particularly interested in what was going on inside me, judging by the way you kept insisting that I ought to know things I'm not even aware I don't know about. For example, how you feel before you say a word about it. According to you, you were fed up with the way our conversations never get where they need to go.

Olivia: No, that isn't even close to what I meant.

Norton: Why am I not surprised by that?

Olivia: Because I don't know if you are capable of surprise. That's a kind of romantic feeling, and I'm not sure you have a romantic bone in your body at this point.

Norton: Well, was there any point at which you thought there was?

Olivia: It's pointless to go there. That moment's come and gone.

Norton: And it's pointless to go back there? It's really too bad you didn't point it out to me when it was here.

Olivia: I'd say so.

Norton: Still, if you want me to understand what you feel, there's no point in giving up on it.

Olivia: No point at all. That's what I said.

Norton: That's what I thought you said. And I think that you were making a good point until you retracted it.

Olivia: So why don't you just make it happen? I've been waiting.

Norton: I know you've been waiting, but I've asked you to meet me halfway and let me know what you want because if I have to guess at it, I can feel my energy draining. This is too important to have to guess about.

Olivia: I never asked you to guess. I need you to know.

Norton: I know that I want to connect with you.

Olivia: Then go ahead.

Norton: I'm trying.

Olivia: Are you really?

Norton: Yes, I really am.

Olivia: Well, that should count for something.

Norton: I'm hoping it does.

Olivia: Well, I think it does.

Norton: All right then. I think we are getting someplace.

Olivia: I knew you'd figure it out. It wasn't so hard really. The fact that you made the effort made all the difference.

Norton: Do you really think so?

Olivia: Yes.

Norton: Well, you ought to know.

Olivia: No, it's you who ought to know.

Norton: Uh oh.

Olivia: I'm starting to have that feeling again.

Norton: Don't tell me. Or better yet. Do. Tell me.

Olivia: That's the whole point. I don't want to have to tell you. I want you to know.

Norton: Oh, I see.

Olivia: Good. Finally.

CHAPTER TWO

Emotional Safety

*Love cures people—both the ones who
give it and the ones who receive it.*

—Karl A. Menninger

Think about this statement for a moment: *With emotional safety, partners can be themselves.* Without emotional safety a person can only be genuinely defensive or angry. *With emotional safety, partners can be themselves* refers to a way partners can be when they are relaxed within. When you say you can "be yourself" with someone, it means you don't have to hide what you really feel. You can make yourself vulnerable. You feel no need to cover up because you are not afraid to be disapproved of, exposed, or ridiculed. You can present yourself as you experience yourself to be without putting on airs or disguises. Now this doesn't mean your partner will always be able to respond to you on the same wavelength you are feeling. But it signifies a basic authenticity within the way you present yourself to your partner. That is what an atmosphere of emotional safety can make possible. If you do not feel emotionally safe with your partner, you protect, rather than expose, much of who you are. Feelings of neglect, isolation, and abandonment develop because the parts of you that are protected are deprived of human contact.

These three questions slow down reactivity and help you create emotional safety in almost any situation:

- ❤ *How are you feeling?* Awareness of how you feel is primary. To speak or act without awareness of how you are feeling is dangerous. To create emotionally safe messages, you must start with an awareness of where you yourself are coming from.

- ❤ *How is your partner feeling?* Think about who your partner is in the moment. Timing is important, although not all communications can be planned. Is he at his best? His worst? Is he likely to have a problem with what you have in mind to discuss? None of these questions necessarily prohibit you from trying to have a dialogue in the moment. The point of mentioning these things is that they are the kind of considerations that can help you decide when the optimal time to get your message across may be. Many issues require ongoing conversation. So the idea is often not to target a time to resolve a particular issue but to find a time to open it for discussion and then work to continue resolving it.

- ❤ *What do you want to accomplish in your conversation?* Having awareness of what you would like to accomplish with your partner is critical to establishing a sense of connection. If you are able to move in the direction you would like, that's great. If the conversation leaves you feeling that your approach was unproductive, you are then in a position to adjust accordingly. This posture—a flexible one—is useful and necessary. It is a sign that the way you approach your partner is nuanced

and mindful of opportunities for learning from experience
rather than blindly plunging into conversation without regard
to the consequences.

On a functional level, emotional safety is equivalent to a standing
invitation to share what is going on inside. Or if the moment prevents
you from doing this, you have the opportunity to make sure at some
time that you can arrange to get the attention you need. Emotional
safety between partners, parent and child, friends, sometimes work
partners, and even, in ideal circumstances, between an individual and
her community can be important.

When we experience emotional safety within ourselves, the most
highly evolved aspects of our capacities for social engagement become
active. This is far from the case when we are feeling defensive or
aggressive.

Feeling emotionally safe results from a process of self-monitoring
called *neuroception*. This largely unconscious process informs our
nervous system as to whether conditions—both within and outside
the self—are safe or unsafe. Depending on whether or not conditions
are felt to be safe, specific neurological functions are either activated
or shut down.

Only when we feel emotionally safe can we invite or emanate
emotional safety in our interpersonal relationships. If we do not
feel safe, whatever we do derives from and is a form of defensive
maneuvering. The difference between listening empathetically and
acting as if you are listening empathetically is subtle but real. It has
to do with whether the listener feels emotionally safe. The "as if"
listener may seem to function well in a relationship from moment
to moment, but, ultimately, the difference between as-if and the real
thing becomes painfully obvious and has consequences within the
relationship. The as-if listener has no vision of genuine intimacy or

closeness. And that counts. This is the difference between a partner who provides lip service and one who responds with heartfelt, thoughtful responses.

We need human contact to survive. At the same time, we are also wired to avoid emotional and all other kinds of danger to survive. The goal of three-dimensional communication is to help partners feel genuinely safe and grounded with each other. Because just as we are wired to connect when we feel safe, we are wired to disconnect when we feel unsafe!

Experiencing emotional safety stimulates expectations that it will be possible to continue to feel safe. Emotional safety creates an upward spiral in which connection, trust, and possibilities for a loving alliance increase. In this respect, emotional safety is a dynamic mind-set. The more regularly you experience emotional safety, the more feelings of loneliness, disconnection, and isolation fade.

Emotional safety experienced within enables heightened capacities for empathy, openness to articulating our feelings, and reading others' feelings. These adaptive functions are not available to us when we are feeling defensive/aggressive.

♥ ♥ ♥

Following is a partial list of common activities or methods that are helpful in developing a state of mind conducive to producing, maintaining, and sharing emotional safety within:

1) Basic relaxation exercises
2) Good nutrition
3) Meditation
4) Breathing exercises
5) Yoga
6) Physical exercise

7) Learning challenges

8) Mental exercises that strengthen focus

Back to Carole and Jim

What was the most intimate understanding the couple still shared as our work began to go forward? Ironically, it was the realization that in their relationship that had started with such high hopes, neither was able to soothe their own or their partner's suffering. Rather than being understood as a force that was tearing down their relationship, if both partners mutually recognized that they were in their separate ways distressed by the lack of connection, might this help reunite them? Could this point of commonality—shared sorrow—help them snap out of the trancelike negativity that had enveloped them?

Carole said, "We keep missing each other."

I asked Jim what he thought about that statement. "That's true. I can't argue with that."

I said, "You could if you wanted to. But I'm glad to hear that you're not interested in doing that. Being able to agree, to see each other's side in little things as well as bigger issues is a choice. Of course, it's easier to acknowledge the other's side of things when there is no conflict because you look into the 'other' side, the side within your partner, and see what you see within yourself. But it's also important to nurture the ability to see into the other's side of things when you are not in agreement."

Anatomy of an Argument

Carole then brought up a disagreement that had escalated into a disheartening quarrel. During a time that she and Jim were driving Nora, their daughter, to her friend's house, Carole had asked Jim to drive more slowly.

"If she can come up with a way to criticize what I'm doing, she will," Jim said. "I don't know why she does it, but it annoys me. I'm no psychologist, but I think she does it to put herself above me."

Dangers of Certainty

Jim believed Carole felt a need to be in control and, therefore, needed him to feel "in the wrong," or out of control. Jim responded to this with either a counterattack, a countercriticism, or by giving Carole the "silent treatment." Either way left them both feeling alone and misunderstood.

During these clashes, he saw Carole as an adversary. And he'd consistently interpret whatever she'd say in this way. In each argument, he looked for and identified something in Carole's words that confirmed his view that she was trying to hurt him. Since he was focused on finding this common thread, his ability to notice anything she said that reflected, for example, a desire to make peace and reconnect was impaired.

To a disarming degree, we find what we look for. In seeing Carole as an adversary, Jim completely overlooked another perspective. Even during this argument, Carole was trying to highlight her need to feel connected with him, safe with him, heard by him. He was oblivious to these themes in their dialogue because he was preoccupied with defending himself from the hostility he expected.

Jim made assumptions about what lay beneath Carole's words—the second dimension. Staying too literal, staying in the first dimension as Jim tended to do, caused him to miss the second, and he rarely ever tuned in to or was aware of the third dimension of their communication.

What became clear as we worked together was that he was not aware that he was being reactive. He felt that he was just being himself. And he intuited that being himself involved only one way of responding, the way that came reflexively to him. He eventually saw how it could be considered defensive. That was a breakthrough for him and helped move our work along considerably.

Food for Thought: Does this sound familiar? Do you know people who excuse their hostile or unfriendly behavior on the grounds that it "comes naturally," that it is "just the way I am"? What do you think about this explanation? in terms of thinking three-dimensionally, can you see how this explanation misses the point entirely? Where is any concern or aware-ness of emotional safety in it? What about the expression, "This is the way I express myself. I can't help it if I am the way I am." That makes some sense. The question is, are you interested in learning more about communication than you already know? Do you think it might help you? That it might help your relationship? What we know before working to build emotional safety can take us a long way, but the vast majority of us need to keep learning and growing if we want to attain secure attachment with our partners. Think about these questions in relation to your partner. Also, think about them in relation to yourself. These questions are an essential part of a mindful exploration of communication.

How could Jim have tempered his anger and teased out other feel-ings that might have been driving him? And what would those other feelings be?

My expectation that Jim was saddened and felt lonely as a result of the chronic conflicts with Carole was later revealed. But this aspect of his own feelings was invisible to him because his anger camou-flaged them. The emotional range he responded to within himself was constricted. He was unaware of the broader continuum of his feel-ings. We can compare this to a thermometer that accurately measures temperatures above a certain degree-mark and then below another degree-mark but has no capacity to differentiate temperatures that fall in between those benchmarks. He accurately read his extreme temperatures, but anything in the middle range was a blur. Let's carry further the metaphor of the thermometer to Jim's acknowledgment of his feelings. Those corresponding to extreme events registered: he was joyous at the birth of his child and tearful at the death of a relative, while everyday emotions were hard for him to notice or differentiate. Although this condition is arguably more common in men, it affects women as well.

My intention here is to describe how and why defensive hostility became Jim's go-to response. But it takes two to lock into a dysfunctional communication pattern. Let's take a look at Carole's part in this.

Where's the Third Dimension Here?

Here's how Carole felt about her communication with Jim: "Jim's anger, and the way he seems to always find something to be angry about, shows that he is unaware of so much of who I am in our relationship. I feel like I'm invisible to him. And that is painful. It leaves me feeling invisible myself. I feel alone a lot of the time we are together. I'm beginning to believe that he doesn't care about me. And that really hurts. I haven't felt that before."

Their dilemma was that they could not escape the pain of isolation. This was true because the source of the warmth and love they both needed was also the source of their bruised feelings and need for comforting: each other. And Carole was oblivious to the fact that they *both* were experiencing that disconnection. The question I needed to address was, what will it take to help them make a breakthrough?

CHAPTER THREE

Anger and Its Triggers

Any problem, big or small, within a family,
always seems to start with bad communication.
Someone isn't listening.

—Emma Thompson

When we started working together, Jim became aware of his anger only at the point at which he was already acting it out. By that time, much damage to trust had been suffered in the form of unfriendly remarks, frosty silences.

Many are surprised to learn that a lot of anger is caused by frustrated attachment needs. How does this make sense? People who are dissatisfied with their own or their partner's communication (or with both) become enraged because their attachment needs go unmet. And that, in turn, triggers feelings of insecurity and loneliness.

Much of the conversation we typically associate with relational turmoil—blaming and accusations, detailed grievances of the other's shortcomings, descriptions of their annoying traits and disappointing responses—is misconstrued. By and large these grievances are not the real deal breakers. These issues are symptomatic of a couple's inability to create emotional safety and resolve differences. These are categories of problems—like snoring or eye-rolling or even poor listening skills—that can often be solved with creative ingenuity. The deeper frustration is the inability to communicate about them. That is what causes the rifts that tear apart hopes, dreams, and relational bonds. Not having a three-dimensional communication pattern in place is like being a wondrous organism full of life and potential that lacks an immune system. A minor cut can result in a deadly infection. Partners who have enough attraction and perseverance to join each other and commit to working out a relationship resemble this helpless and hapless organism if their communication process doesn't work. After the initial burst of relational momentum—the honeymoon phase—dies down, partners easily fall prey to dysfunctional communication patterns. At best, a dysfunctional pattern allows partners to avoid dealing with the problems that threaten to overwhelm them. Once the partners run out of room for avoidance, the dysfunction dissipates whatever trust has been preserved. That is, unless the couple can develop emotional safety. Because that is what they'd need to resolve, rather than avoid, their issues.

The recipient of anger, caused by one partner's frustration at not being able to connect with the other, commonly interprets the expression of anger as a personal rejection. Often this is a misinterpretation. Angry partners very often reject the state and structure of the communication that has developed between themselves and their partner, not the person who seems to be the object of their anger! This is because instead of connecting to the partner, dysfunctional communication, as we discussed in the first chapter, is not only ineffective, it makes improved communication impossible. Dysfunctional communication prevents connection because it is designed to serve a defensive purpose. It blocks the flow of information and emotion because contact in a dysfunctional relationship can be toxic, and measures, like dysfunctional communication, are set in place to prevent the damage that can result from allowing a toxic message to penetrate. And if the dysfunction goes on too long, it becomes increasingly difficult to break out of this pattern.

The distinction drawn above can help you lower the intensity of angry exchanges in most everyday situations because for many couples, *faulty communication patterns, not your partner, pose the most immediate threat to the well-being of your relationship.* This distinction also leads you to realize that you need your partner's cooperation and energy to create a better connection. It is not something you can achieve on your own.

At least temporarily relieved of the onus of rejection, partners can look more carefully at the triggers that led up to their angry outbursts when they embrace this perspective on anger. The more Jim began to understand the signs that he was becoming angry, the better able he was to curtail destructive outbursts. He could control making counterattacks when he felt criticized. He learned to ask questions instead of firing back the first thing that came to mind. He learned to understand that most of the time Carole's criticisms contained a desire for connection under the surface, in that second dimension. After a while, he shifted his focus. He began to look for invitations to connect. If he hadn't been looking for them, it's doubtful whether he would have found them.

Instead of feeling deflated and defensive when Carole edged into a critical statement, Jim was coached to feel needed. He was encouraged to *interpret* what had been perceived as criticism as a call for help, a cry of frustration at not being able to connect. As Jim softened, Carole followed suit. This is how anger cycles de-escalate. Awareness of the underlying attachment issue had a soothing effect on both partners. The third dimension took root in their communication process as a result of these changes.

Jim started to be able to hold himself accountable for things that he needed to work on. Number one was his temper and the certainty with which he had held the assumption that Carole had wanted him to feel bad.

Carole looked Jim in the eye and appealed to him to believe that she did not want him to feel bad about himself, that she wanted him to feel good, in fact. Her statement made in a private setting also had public resonance because a third person witnessed it: me. Sometimes a straightforward declaration can take on the power of a ceremonial vow. It seemed to with this couple.

There are times when written words also gain power for some of the same reasons. We associate written communication with public statement, and this can increase the charge of what is being communicated. I recommended that Jim and Carole supplement their verbal communication with notes to each other about their feelings for each other and their relationship. Although most of what they said to each other they had verbalized, it seemed that sometimes they were able to get a particular point across by writing about it, whereas speaking about it had not achieved the desired effect. Carole left reminders for Jim that she appreciated certain things he had done around the house and with Nora, their daughter. These served to bolster the meta-message that she wanted him to hear: she appreciated him. Both partners wrote and received notes from the other and reported feeling good about it.

If note-writing is something you do not do regularly, this exercise can be valuable for you.

Think of a simple statement you would like your partner to take in and think about. Something that proclaims your feeling and that you'd like him to consider taking to heart.

Make it something you feel he doesn't grasp in the way you'd like him to at present. But let it be something you think would further connection. Make it positive. Include the message in a note. E-mail is okay, but an old-fashioned paper-and-pencil note sometimes works even better.

For example, you might write something like this if this fits your situation and you feel this way: "We've been arguing a lot lately. I am confident we will work things out. Please remember I love you no matter how much we argue." A note like that can ease insecurity.

Think about a message that would further the development of emotional safety for you and your partner. Make it about something you would like him to take to heart.

A second approach to this exercise is to think about a note you would like to receive. Identify the feeling your note would produce in you. Now try to focus on what kind of message it would take to produce that or a similar feeling in your partner. Write that note and leave it for your partner. This is a good exercise for stimulating your creativity, your ability to put yourself in your partner's place, and your ability to clarify what you would like to hear your partner say or write to you. And, of course, what you believe your partner might want to hear or read.

These changes in the couple's communication process greatly reduced the frequency of Carole's feeling that Jim did not care for her anymore. Reciprocally, Jim no longer felt that Carole was looking for things to criticize about him to bring him down. Each felt more valued by the other.

Becoming Mindful of Doubts

Many partners feel unprepared for the learning that goes into developing three-dimensional communication. They are skeptical of their ability to achieve it. Some flat out do not believe themselves capable of making these changes. Do you feel this way? The importance of negative expectation cannot be overestimated. And the importance of believing that negative expectation cannot be overcome? Even more so.

On page 64, you can complete an exercise designed to help you assess the degree of confidence you have in your capacity to make effective use of three-dimensional communication skills to improve your relationship.

Your openness or lack of openness to the possibility of succeeding will temper your resilience in going through the change process that leads to achieving three-dimensional communication. Learning from mistakes in itself is a key element in the culture of open communication. And opening up to possibilities for forgiveness—only if earned and appropriate—also can be nurtured by awareness of how possible you believe positive change is for yourself and your partner. Think about this: Some partners carry anger toward themselves for feeling unable to be more optimistic about making the changes needed to improve their relationship. On top of the anger, they also feel ashamed that they feel this way. This exacerbates their anger. In addition, they may believe they are weak for having these feelings. What would it take to forgive themselves for having these feelings? What would it take for them to allow themselves to view their anger and shame as a distraction from getting on with the work to be done in improving communication? What would it take to feel compassionate toward *themselves* for being under so much pressure to make changes? If you identify with any part of this cascade of feelings, I have a recommendation for you. Take a leap over to the issue of self-compassion and focus on it. The path to three-dimensional communication is strewn with compassion. Consider viewing it that way. And accept that the atmosphere of generosity that you need to feel emotionally safe has to include a component of self-compassion to power it. Self-compassion is the ticket out of any difficulties similar to the ones just described.

Having hope and confidence that your relationship with your partner will go well is an enviable, but far from typical, outlook for couples experiencing relational distress. Working to consciously preserve or resuscitate a sense of *possibility* that the relationship can improve is a valuable objective worth striving to achieve.

It takes courage to intentionally open yourself to possibilities for healing in a relationship that has been disappointing. If you open yourself to the possibility of feeling hopeful, no one can offer any guarantees that you will not be disappointed again. However, it is just this risk that allows you to avoid being preoccupied with defending yourself or attacking your partner. Being able to risk feeling hopeful enables you to stay attuned to opportunities for positive change as they present themselves. If you are completely closed to possibilities of hopefulness, these may well prove impossible to detect, much less act upon.

Tips for Increasing Doubt Awareness

Slowing down enough to address skepticism or cynicism about change and bringing it into awareness can help to soften it.

Bringing doubts to awareness, being mindful of doubts, promotes possibilities for optimism about improving your communication process.

Can you take time to think about doubts you entertain about whether you can improve your communication process with your partner? What do you anticipate will be the largest obstacles?

List reasons, whether practical, emotional, or based on past experience, that might interfere with you and your partner making headway with communication. Make two copies of that list. Put one away in a drawer so that you can refer to it and remind yourself what you are trying to rise above.

Take the second copy of the list and devise a ritual of letting go that will symbolize the possibility of being free of these obstacles. You can shred it or burn it. You can scatter torn pieces of it in a way that will be memorable for you. Of course, you can bury those pieces of doubts, fears, and obstacles. You can attach them to helium-filled balloons and let them go outside!

The idea is that you can handle these challenges in a manner in which you feel some degree of control. This is not magic. This is a method of growing accustomed to the idea that these issues can be managed.

It will take time before you can actually scatter your communication problems to the wind or ignite them into oblivion, but it can be helpful to experience this as a ritual of readiness to grow beyond the list of identifiable problems you now face.

When we try to do something in a new way, like when we try to improve communication, we unconsciously flinch at the prospect of becoming someone different from how we understand ourselves to be. Fear of the unknown is triggered because we are not sure and have only limited control, if any, over who we are becoming. We become genuinely new to ourselves as we go through changes, which can be exhilarating or terrifying or sometimes both.

Slowing Down the Communication

Carole asked Jim to slow down the car. He declared, "You know, it's important for me to feel comfortable when I'm driving. Your criticisms of my driving puts me on edge, which is not a safe situation for us. Why are you doing this to me?"

Jim felt victimized and was on the defensive about what he interpreted as Carole's criticism of his driving. He read her words in a certain way without considering the possibility that the message—her goal and desire—behind her words might have been to connect with him, not to alienate him: to reach out to him, not to insult him.

Meanwhile, two thoughts were uppermost in Carole's mind at the time this argument was developing in the car between them. The first was that she felt a headache coming on and that, for some reason she could not explain, if the car was moving at a more leisurely pace she believed the pain might lessen. The second reason had to do with Nora. Carole regularly had panicky feelings when the child was riding in her car seat, and she was feeling that if the car should stop short, Nora would be hurt. Given the circumstances, Carole understood that the threat of imminent danger to their daughter was very small. Nonetheless, she thought it would soothe her anxiety, rational or not, if Jim slowed down the car. All in all, her wish to slow the car might have been a displacement of a wish that Jim would help her cope with her angst.

Jim's interpretation of Carole's words as criticism crowded out mindful attention to here and now information, like whether or not her tone was hostile, contentious, or contemptuous. He heard her words and presumed they were coming from a perspective that in some way found him wanting. Close attention to the tone of Carole's voice may have helped Jim evaluate the second and third dimension of what Carole was saying as something other than criticism. But his ire was aroused quickly, and he did not have the presence of mind to differentiate her tone of voice from the attitude he presumed her words were expressing. He was convinced that Carole was attacking his sense of confidence in being in control of his vehicle. He saw her as competing with him for control of the vehicle, even though he was the driver.

According to Carole, she had not been hostile, contentious, or con-temptuous. Admittedly, her presentation was oblique. Instead of ask-ing for support in slowing herself down, she requested he slow down the vehicle. But experience dictates that partners need to anticipate that what seems to be one kind of a communication may really con-tain another. Often embedded within a seeming criticism is a wish for help and connection. Even the rolling of the eyes can indicate not simply contempt for the speaker but a feeling of helplessness about not being able to respond in a more useful, constructive manner. Meaning depends on context. Gestures can express more than one feeling at a time as well.

Partners can't be expected to read between the lines all the time, but reading between the lines, separating something that looks like a distancing maneuver from an embedded wish to be understood better, is and does become part of what it sometimes takes to enter a process of renewal.

Is it completely foreign to the way you and your partner talk to each other now? If so, consider making a conscious effort to look beneath the first dimension and identify whether a bid for connection may be lurking within a remark that might otherwise have sounded like a criticism or disinterested statement.

When they don't know what to say, some partners say things they either don't mean or wish they hadn't said. In hindsight they learn that their remarks moved the conversation away from where they wanted it to go. For example, some partners make clumsy comments and regret them not only for their clumsiness but also because they failed to capture what they had wished to convey. So they spoke poorly, left themselves open to misinterpretation, and, on top of that, the message they did not wish to convey was hurtful. Disentangling a confused and mangled communication process can and does entail involvement in some messy and less than clear-cut conversation. The third dimension—the dimension of mindfulness and possibility—lies beyond the mess. In order to get there, the mess has to be acknowledged and worked through.

Jim hadn't shared his thoughts about feeling demeaned or controlled. Carole had not shared her thoughts or feelings about the oncoming headache or her anxieties about Nora. Do you think it might have made a difference if they had shared these things? I asked them each this question.

Jim said that if he had been asked to slow down because Carole felt a headache coming on and told that the slowdown might help her, he could have slowed down and felt good about it. He said that he would probably not have felt criticized if he knew how Carole was feeling. "It would have made a big difference," he said.

For her part, Carole stated that if Jim had let her know he felt criticized by her request to slow down, she would have explained that she had a headache and that she was not being critical of his driving or his judgment as a driver. "At least that's the way I would have liked to handle it if I were self-possessed enough to say it that way," she said. If she had known he was taking her request as a criticism, "I would have wanted to make sure I helped him see it differently," she said.

In-Between Talk

Often what people mean when they say their communication is poor is that these kinds of second-dimension, in-between messages do not get voiced, and partners are left to make assumptions or presumptions about the other's motives for saying and doing what they say and do.

Reflection is not a frill that can be added on to the communication process now and again. It needs to be installed the way a new operating system in a computer gets put into place and runs all the time, if not in the foreground then in the background.

Has the following question occurred to you?

A person I was working with asked, "Well, if I'm always comparing the way things are to the way they could or should be, then it would get pretty depressing because the way things are doesn't measure up."

Although I can understand this person's point, those underlying feelings of depression won't go away by themselves. They must be dealt with, and the first step in dealing with them is to be aware they are there and then work them through.

Falling into a pitfall of perfectionism can develop from this awareness, and that comes with its own set of difficulties. The constructive purpose of awareness of a discrepancy between where you are and where you want to be as a couple is to motivate, not flagellate, yourself or your partner. It may be discouraging to realize you have a long way to go to be where you'd like to be with your partner *unless* you can recognize that embedded in that insight is the wish to bridge that distance. The wish for the relationship to support this insight can signal the beginning of envisioning positive changes, including more emotional safety. If you and your partner can mutually agree that you both want things to be better than they are, you have the foundation for teamwork in making this happen. This is an important and necessary benchmark in the healing process.

The price for shutting down awareness of how much work remains to be done is that you lose the opportunity to notice not only how deep the problems in the relationship are but, more important, forfeit noticing when things are getting better! Think of it as a monitoring screen on a large control panel that helps direct your relationship. If this screen is dark, you are traveling blind and lose track not only of your own way but of whether you are in harm's way. How can you develop confidence in your communication process if you can't reflect clearly on it? The only thing you could do to develop confidence while using avoidant strategies would be to avoid dealing with what is in front of you. And who needs that? Masters of evasion and masters of connection are two mutually exclusive groups.

To focus your reflective capacity so that you do not torture yourself by continuously feeling you are not doing as well as you need to, it's important to adopt these two parameters for focus: 1) the positive, and 2) the possible. Identifying where these parameters begin and end in your life is not always easy. But it is important. Why isn't it easy? Because interpersonal relationships are not easy; they are complex, complicated, and multidimensional. That is the way it is. Once you accept life's complexities, you can at times simplify issues and create a genuine sense of control and optimism because you feel less overwhelmed by complexity. It is one of the wonderful by-products of a full-hearted acceptance of life's richness. And by richness I mean dazzle and brilliance but also its difficulty.

COMMUNICATION MINI-EXERCISE:
Three-dimensional clarity checkpoint:
First dimension: Did you say what you meant?
Second dimension: Have you conveyed what you wanted to convey in terms of intensity, coloring, and emotional tone?
Third dimension: Have you considered what the message may open up or shut down in your communication process? Have you thought about that in terms of yourself *and* your partner?

The Why and the Why-Now Factors

Clarity in communication has to do with giving messages enough context so that your partner not only knows what you are telling or asking him but also has a sense of *why* you are asking and what it says about how you feel about what is happening either in the relationship or within yourself at the time. Helping your partner understand why you are giving the message you are giving and why you are giving it *now* are two key factors in keeping your dialogue emotionally safe. Clarity in communication hinges on mutual understanding of the *Why and Why-Now* aspect of dialogue. Surprises can be fun, particularly on joyous occasions. But continuous surprises in communication are usually unnerving. If your partner has a sense of why you are saying what you are saying and why you are saying it now, you are connecting.

If your partner says or does something that causes anger, does it elicit a knee-jerk response from you? Have you put any thought into how you would like to respond when you get angry? If you wait until the moment is upon you, you likely will not have a choice. So it pays to think about this sequence ahead of time. Is this useful advice for you or your partner? You can interrupt the pattern of reactivity. But it requires devoting some attention to the problem.

Food for thought: A knee-jerk response is based on a split-second *interpretation* of what your partner's action means to you. That is to say, your interpretation of the meaning not only of his action but what was behind that action. Your knee-jerk response stems from a primitive survival mechanism. When humans lived in the wild, it often was imperative that they respond immediately. A quick reaction on an everyday basis could be the difference between life and death. Civilization has made the predominance of this sort of response a dysfunctional liability in everyday couples' lives. Because contrary to days of old, very little that happens between partners rises to a life-and-death need for an immediate response. In our contemporary lives we not only have the luxury to give ourselves time to consider options, we have the freedom to view solutions as part of a process and not merely an instantaneous survival event. Your mate may cross you and cause you to *feel* like you are being attacked by a saber-toothed tiger, but in the twenty-first century this is a metaphor for how you feel, not the reality of your survival needs.

So we need to work with our vestigial orientation to challenge. Our exquisite neurological capacity, geared to help us survive harsh adversity, needs to be adjusted from the forest and jungle rules of survival to the apartment or house, urban or suburban, twenty-first-century domicile.

When confronted with this reality, that our biology has not caught up with conditions of our contemporary lives, many say, "I feel the way I feel because it is the way I'm made. That can't be tampered with."

It may surprise you to note that the approach I recommend fits very well with this attitude. Because what I'm saying is that these feelings that "I am the way I am and that's that" have a legitimate place in your psyche and personality. They are legitimate and worthy of respect. But to the extent that this way of thinking is limiting, they are a hindrance. The "I gotta be me" that signifies "I have a temper, I was born that way, and it's natural for me to act as I do" is not in question. The question is, were you also born to work with other capabilities that you possess? And were you born with the potential to modify those capacities as survival dictates? Research shows that people survive longer when paired, particularly in satisfying relationships. In her book *For Better: The Science of Twenty-First Century Marriage*, Tara Parker-Pope writes of the numerous health benefits of marriages that achieve good communication processes. Major health indicators, like blood pressure, heart functionality, and longevity, improve. And these relationships are not based on the idea that people are stuck with their biological predilections, but on the supposition that these characteristics, within reasonable parameters, are modifiable.

We've had successive generations of breakthroughs in understanding our neurological heritage, but interpersonally we are only starting to understand the basis for our more primitive behaviors as well as for our most-evolved cortical and interpersonal capacities.

Among the most important of these advanced features is our *reflective capacity*—our ability to regulate our feelings sufficiently to consider our options before taking action. Learning to integrate our reflective capacity into how we treat one another, which is the basis of three-dimensional communication, stands as our current personal, interpersonal, and cultural-communal challenge.

Gaining access to this reflective capacity as we grapple with difficult interpersonal challenges is the subject of this book. As far as couples' relationships go, this involves learning to bring out the best in one another.

This signifies nurturing your liveliest and most creative potential, not to mention your happiest. Achieving this on a social level prepares us for a world in which mutual support, cooperation, and creativity are the norm.

Twenty-First Century Anger Management

Throughout most of the twentieth century, therapists encouraged patients to vent their anger as a way of relieving the stress caused by keeping feelings bottled up. From popular songs to pop psychology to consulting rooms all over America, "letting it all hang out" was hailed as a sophisticated, natural, and healthful release. It turns out that policies that qualify as sophisticated and natural sometimes turn out to be short-sighted and harmful. Contemporary research informs us that venting anger increases the tendency to vent rather than relieving the reservoir of anger. In other words, the more involved with angry responses you are, the more anger you feel. And the more you interpret your feelings as having a connection to anger, the less likely you are to clearly identify other emotions. Anger becomes dominant not only in terms of which emotions are expressed but also in terms of which emotions are recognized as real. Anger can then dominate the emotional landscape. *Uninhibited release of anger* creates the tendency toward intermittent explosiveness disorder. And that is problematic, if not devastating, in relationships.

Denial of anger is not the desired alternative. Neither is suppression of anger. Choosing how to release and when to release anger is key. Another way to describe this phenomenon is being mindful of anger. Relief from anger requires understanding and soothing. Anger is a signal that someone is in pain, needs attention, or feels that something is wrong. What needs to follow from an expression of anger is that the pain, the need for attention, or the feeling that something is wrong is being taken seriously and addressed. That is the key to twenty-first-century anger management. Although there is nothing very complicated or confusing about this notion, it contradicts ideas about handling anger that many of us have grown up with. Many of us associate the expression of anger with an event, such as getting something off your chest or even finally getting even, rather than with a process that has steps and leads to connection as well as, at times, interpersonal justice, as opposed to simple catharsis.

Do you have difficulty identifying or expressing anger appropriately? Do you have difficulty figuring out what an appropriate expression of anger would be? One strategy that can help is to anticipate that when your anger is triggered, or if you sense it may be under the surface, there *may* be a reason behind your partner's action or statement that is different from the one you've registered. In other words, consciously connect the feeling of anger or the suspicion that you may be getting angry with *curiosity* about what is going on. Obviously, this technique first slows down the reactive process and gives you an additional moment to consider whether the statement or request that made you angry could have been made for a reason other than the one you focused on. *Could it have meant something other than what you took it to mean?* This has the added benefit of leading you to reflect on whether what you are angry about is worth getting angry about, even if you find it annoying. Second, even if you deem anger to be appropriate to what has happened, you get to consider your response rather than simply reacting on autopilot.

In emergency situations, this slowed-down anger response may not make sense. The point is that we *misinterpret* many situations as emergency—saber-toothed tiger sightings—when they need to be understood otherwise!

Make Self-Focus the Focus

Self-focus is the crux of relationship change. Focusing on attempts to force your partner to make changes is a road map to relational hell.

Not only does it never work but also it is a distraction from doing the work that can be done that might help bring your relationship into a state of connection. The big changes you want to see in your relationship begin with changes *within yourself.*

Please note that I am talking about changes within the relationship. If you or your partner is abusive, this is a different story. Abuse must be curtailed as soon as possible. It is never productive to tolerate it. And self-focus in situations involving abuse translates into self-protection. It is not defensiveness when you protect yourself from abuse; it is self-respect. (See Appendix 5, If Abuse Is the Issue, for resources countering abuse.)

EXERCISE 3.1

Confidence Quiz
Rate Your Confidence in Making
Your Relationship Better

How we approach healing in a relationship has a powerful effect on how much healing we are able to accomplish. If you have confidence that you will learn what you need to know and use it to improve your relationship, the chances are that you will.

If you lack that confidence, it's important to be aware of it and work on strengthening it. This quiz will help you evaluate your confidence in taking what you learn and having it make the difference you need it to make.

Please rate each item with a score of 1 to 5.

1 = No Confidence; **2** = Very Little Confidence; **3** = No Comment;
4 = Mild Confidence; **5** = Certainty

1) Do you have confidence that your partner would do his part to improve your relationship to the full extent that he understood the role he needed to play?

1   2   3   4   5

2) Will your partner persevere in figuring out what she needs to do to make your relationship work?

1   2   3   4   5

3) How much credence do you give to the possibility that you will put in a sincere effort to make whatever changes you need to make in order to create an adequate level of emotional safety for yourself and your partner?

1   2   3   4   5

4) How much faith do you have in the possibility that you will figure out whatever you need to learn to bring out your partner's most loving potential?

1   2   3   4   5

5) Do you believe that you and your partner, as a team, will create and maintain emotional safety within your relationship?

1   2   3   4   5

6) How much credibility would you give this statement: "I can learn to identify what triggers my partner's anger and use that information to significantly reduce the number and intensity of unproductive conversations we have"?

1   2   3   4   5

7) How would you rate the probability of this happening: "My partner can learn to identify what triggers my anger and use that information to reduce the number and intensity of unproductive conversations we have"?

1   2   3   4   5

8) Neither I nor my partner will give up on trying to make our relationship as good as it can be.

1   2   3   4   5

9) Can you imagine you and your partner being able to defuse "hot button" topics—like money, sex, or whatever is else hard for you to discuss—to the extent that you use conversations on these topics to learn about each other without intensifying tensions in the relationship?

1   2   3   4   5

10) How would you rate the chance that you and your partner accept each other with a loving and compassionate spirit, even when you find you have issues about which you probably will never agree?

1   2   3   4   5

♥ ♥ ♥

Scoring Instructions:

Add the points from items 1 through 10. **Final Score:** _____

Results Analysis:

If your score is within the range of 41 to 50: You trust that you and your partner are up to the task of healing whatever difficulties you are having in your communication. You stand an excellent chance of making great progress in healing your relationship difficulties.

If your score is within the range of 33 to 40: You have limited confidence in your relationship. You have not given up on making it work in ways that are important to you. It is important that you face areas of difference or disagreement with compassion and curiosity.

If your score is within the range of 20 to 32: You probably vacillate between feeling hopeful and despairing about working through problems. It is possible that you are unclear about your own motivation to heal your relationship with your partner. The feeling of disconnection, discouragement, and disillusion are probably strong, but you have moments of connection as well. You have nothing to lose by throwing yourself wholeheartedly into doing your part to open up communication. It is likely that your dialogue with your partner bears no resemblance to three-dimensional communication patterns at present. Focus on establishing emotional safety. You may find there is much more to your relationship than you ever imagined.

If your score is within the range of 0 to 19: In many ways you have already checked out of your relationship. Still, if you were able to establish three-dimensional communication, think about what it is and how you might be able to know your partner on a deeper level than either of you have experienced together. Given the stress level, you may be surprised to learn how much yearning for emotional safety exists under the surface of the relationship; likely this is invisible to you both.

What you can accomplish is based to a significant degree on how you define your stance as you approach solving a problem. When the problem involves improving your relationship, taking stock of your faith in your own and your partner's ability to make necessary changes is crucial. If you believe that either you or your partner is not up to the task, your approach will be constricted, your ability to rebound from minor setbacks diminished, and your willingness to persevere reduced.

Assessing your belief in your partner's ability to come through for you can make the critical difference between going through the motions of trying to create effective communication and actually creating effective communication.

Should this quiz indicate that you have given up on your partner, you will have attained valuable information that you can use to arm yourself against allowing this attitude to become a self-fulfilling prophecy. If you lack confidence in your partner or yourself, awareness of that lack of confidence is needed to make sure you do not prematurely write off opportunities for healing before giving them their due. Lack of confidence can easily extend to lack of willingness to allow for the possibility that breakthroughs may occur. Without openness to the possibility that things can improve, likelihood that they will get better declines.

CHAPTER FOUR

What's Willingness Got to Do with It?

Communication leads to community,
that is, to understanding, intimacy,
and mutual valuing.

—Rollo May

What's Willingness?

Carole asked Jim to slow down the car. Carole felt alone with uncomfortable feelings. She wanted Jim to help her regulate the anxiety she was feeling. Along with asking him to slow the car, she was hoping to get him to help her slow down her anxiety, as we have discussed earlier.

His slowing down the car would have signified *willingness* to allow her to have an impact on his decision-making process.

We often regulate *things* and sometimes try to influence others as a stand-in for regulating ourselves, particularly when we feel stressed, anxious, or depressed. As it happened, Jim's refusal to slow the car exemplified a lack of support and an increase in anxiety for Carole. If he had slowed down the car, a subtle connection between the two might have been strengthened. Even if she felt anxious, Carole would not have felt anxious *and* alone, which makes a huge difference.

Dialectical Thinking

Jim at first interpreted Carole's asking him to slow down as criticism. He interpreted her request to mean that she thought he was a less than competent driver. We have discussed the view that her remark might have symbolized her wish to connect with him in order to alleviate her anxiety and feel less alone. Often partners hold contradictory interpretations of the same events. Carole's request that he slow the car does not have one absolute meaning. The view that includes both of the partners' interpretations can be called the inclusive or, sometimes, the dialectical perspective. If considered in a compassionate light, the space between their conflicting views offers possibilities for healing. Let's investigate how this is so.

Dialectical thinking is key to being able to explore the possibility that the way we approach something—for example, feeling stuck—may not be the only or the best way to think about it. This suggests that when we feel stuck, it is very often because we are not able to shift into thinking of our situation in a way that would be more helpful to us, in a way that would open up possibilities for us to feel unstuck. That's the dialectic, thinking of one thing in two ways and seeing a relationship between the two. Feeling stuck and being stuck are far from identical. Much of the time, feeling stuck can be overcome. Dialectical thinking can help.

Translate this into thinking about emotional danger. Part of what we feel when we experience a lack of emotional safety is that we may not be able to escape feeling unsafe. After all, if the lack of safety is perceived as easily overcome, it presents only an insignificant problem.

For us to feel that creating emotional safety is a real problem, or even that it might be impossible to achieve, further impedes our ability to think or act creatively to change things for the better. It can be energizing to employ *dialectical thinking*. For example, "Because I feel emotionally unsafe with my partner *does not* mean that I will be unable to work out a creative solution to our problems." Research shows that an optimistic perspective can make the difference between being able to survive under adverse circumstances and perishing. Optimism is not a "trick of the mind"; it is a legitimate survival skill.

Emotion itself requires a symbolic vehicle of some kind to carry its meaning. Whether it is a kiss, a gift, a look of affection, an act of kindness, a word, or a phrase, love (and every other emotion) is transferred through symbolic means. Romance needs symbols. The fulfillment of human potential has to do with more than material survival; it has to do with *communication*—successful manipulation of symbols. Making the effort and exerting the mindfulness necessary to access your partner's code—their way of expressing feelings—requires willingness to reflect, identify, and integrate the symbols that emerge within your way of being together as a couple. The communications that emerge carry your mutual need for connection within. If your partner asks for help with something, sometimes it means she really needs your expertise or physical presence or companionship. Sometimes it simply means she wants to know that you care enough to connect with her in a companionable manner. Rather than seeing this sort of thing as a manipulation, can you accept it as a bid for connection and appreciate it on that level? Sometimes, willingness to do just that can make a huge difference in creating a sense of safety between partners. Willingness to step outside your comfort zone can signify an act of generosity. Allowing your partner to exercise initiative in approaching a situation in a way that may differ from what would occur to you can signify acceptance, even if you think her approach might be less efficient. To assure that your partner feels loved, you must explore what actions carry special meaning for her.

Engaging in this kind of thinking frees us to organize the complexity of interpersonal experience in the service of what will energize feeling mutually connected, respected, and protected. We can deal with the way things are in the moment while still holding in mind the way they can become! The willingness to do this is an affirmation of the importance of the relationship.

This perspective helps us appreciate possibilities for emotional safety even *before* they have surfaced. How? Because we are looking for them. Why? Because we are striving to create them. And we need to be able to do just that if we are not experiencing emotional safety in the present. This is one of the ways we understand that we can bring possibilities alive in the present, even when they are not immediately obvious—because they don't exist *yet*. In other words, if we are feeling disconnected in the moment, we can intentionally think of times we have felt connected in the past and ways we need to be connected in the future. We can use that intentional thinking to align the present moment with those positive associations from the past and future. We can seek to expand that theme in our dialogue and interpersonal experience.

Once we establish emotional safety, we can envision stabilizing it. We free ourselves from the one-dimensional realm of appearances. We connect to the possibility that lies beyond the appearance of the way things are. What am I referring to that is beyond the appearance of the way things are? It is the potential for things to be better than they are. That doesn't always show. But because it isn't showing doesn't mean it isn't there. Or that it isn't possible. Embedded within the way things are, we can find the way things can become. A still frame bears information, but when we see it cast amid a series of stills that form a before and after sequence, we go from flat image to narrative in one fell swoop. Context makes the difference. It allows us to detect direction and movement. Context can allow seeing things in three-dimensional terms. At this point I am using the term *three-dimensional* in a way that is *parallel* to the dimensions as I have described them in Chapter One but not identical. I am using the term to describe how flat space, one dimensionality, differs from three dimensionality in time and space in a way that is analogous to the difference between a black-and-white image and a color one. There is vibrancy, an added element that signifies vitality and richness that three dimensionality—in all the ways the term is used—brings to any way of understanding a situation that is more limited than having three dimensions.

A kiss may just be a kiss and a sigh just a sigh; these gestures may signify a true and deep love or something else—it all depends on the larger context. Three-dimensional communication carries us from the facts at hand into the possible meanings that illuminate those facts. Using a three-dimensional perspective we can "see the light" and the light behind the light; we can put things into context. We can see the meanings within meanings. We can appreciate the need we all have to bring love into our lives. We can acknowledge the primacy of our attachment needs.

If either partner feels *alone* with suffering, the *aloneness*, the sense of isolation, worsens the burden. What stands between a pained state of mind and its becoming worse? Many times in life, it is a responsive partner's demonstration of *willingness* to *be there* to share the burden.

Generosity

There are times when this sharing involves doing something that is not *absolutely* necessary, if that something were considered in "practical" terms. But especially *because* the response *is not absolutely* necessary, that act can convey a spirit of generosity. It is not born of necessity but contributed from a well of goodwill and love. The act of generosity validates that such a supply exists! Necessity may be the mother of invention, but a lack of necessity accompanied by an act of goodwill produces a mood of largesse, which can roughly be translated here as emotional safety. The partner who responds with generosity, think of it as loving-kindness, underscores the act's volitional quality. And so the aspect of willingness resounds within the act and within the relationship as a result. Willingness replaces the burden of aloneness with feelings of connection.

If Jim had demonstrated willingness to slow down and consider what Carole might have been reaching for—connection with him as opposed to the wish to cause him to feel criticized—Carole would have felt empowered. Despite feeling isolated and distressed herself, if she had elicited a friendly response rather than the defensive response he did make, she might have overcome feeling isolated.

A generous response of this kind likewise would validate Jim taking her feelings seriously *on her terms*. Sometimes this can be enough to soothe a headache! This is not mystical. It is an aspect of communication that is often overlooked because it doesn't fit into a neat and tidy logical schema. Demonstrations of willingness count!

This doesn't mean that whenever your partner asks you to do anything, no matter how inconvenient or unexpected it may be, that it is always a good thing to accommodate her. Every situation has to be judged on its own merits. However, cooperation on minor issues can be highly *symbolic* of cooperation on larger issues and, therefore, can have a disproportionately powerful impact.

ENVISIONING EXERCISE

Can you imagine the relationship you want to create with your partner? Jot down on paper some of the key characteristics it would include. If you can envision yourself in a situation with your partner in which you are feeling connected, understood, loved, and cherished, describe how you feel and interactions that have helped you to develop feeling this way.

If you feel better able to create this image through drawing, by all means draw the scene. If you feel comfortable neither writing nor drawing, you can still do valuable work by simply imagining it. Now, however you came to this image(s), you have a template of connectedness you can use as a compass to help you move in this direction. Along the way, you may feel that some of what you envision is possible and some may be unrealistic. That's valuable information. Remember the two parameters we are trying to maintain: achieve what is possible and positive.

If your partner is willing to participate in this exercise and you can discuss the results together in a relaxed and open way, this can help you both to understand each other's relational hopes better.

Acts of generosity get carried forward and generate goodwill. Such interactions can begin a positive emotional resonance, reverse a negative one, or even accomplish both simultaneously. Generosity affirms the very subjectivity—the inner world—of each partner. Mutuality becomes the realm of the here and now for couples who are generous with each other. Willingness and generosity are of a piece. In order to develop a trend of generosity in your relationship, you have to be open and willing to do so.

Opportunities Come and Come Again

Because Jim did not in the moment demonstrate this way of thinking about the issue does not mean he is a failure or lacks in generosity as a partner. He needs to look for the *next* opportunity to activate this process. If one thing is predictable about living with a partner, opportunities for demonstrating generosity present themselves constantly! Every day brings new chances. Looking for them actively is the challenge. This is one issue in which the biblical phrase "seek and ye shall find" holds power and grace.

Responsiveness

Research indicates that the single most reliable indicator of future divorce in heterosexual marriages is when wives feel their emotions have no impact on their husbands' perspectives. By the way, I am confident that the essence of this finding holds true for gay, lesbian, and transgender pairings as well. Unfortunately, authoritative studies to date, at least those I've been able to find, including those conducted by John Gottman, have focused exclusively on hetero couples. The universal concept of couples in which one partner feels hopeless at having an impact on the other is doomed.

It's worth thinking about the relationship between *willingness* and *allowing the other to have impact.* There are times when slowing down a car has more to do with demonstrating that your partner has impact on your actions than anything else. Sometimes rather than indulging a feeling that you are being criticized, you can identify a complaint as a golden opportunity to display generosity.

Expanding Empathy and Intentionality

To make progress in turning toward your partner with generosity, you must target that objective. Position yourself in such a way that you recognize and respond positively to your partner's attempts to connect. At the very least, it's important to confirm that you value her effort in trying to connect. This is critical to creating emotional safety.

I said to Carole and Jim, "When we had begun our work together, at first I had the impression that each of you was dismissing what the other was saying before what was said had even registered. Jim, you were convinced Carole manufactured reasons to criticize you so that she would feel superior. While you, Carole, felt that Jim's anger and defensiveness showed a willful disinterest in grasping the emotional need behind what you had said to him. Each of you, using reciprocal stereotyping, were closed to considering that, in spite of what the surface conversation seemed to be about, you both needed connection and neither was finding a way to make it happen. You each retreated into defensive positions. These became self-defeating justifications for maintaining your fears and doubts about the relationship. You were both set up to do battle, not to strengthen connection."

Food for Thought: Does the term *surface conversation* make sense to you? Is it clear that by surface conversation I am referring to the first dimension of your communication? Do you understand that the idea of three-dimensional communication is that, for communication to nourish your relationship, it must include what is happening on the surface but also consider what is going on under the surface?

I continued. "However, as we have talked about how the conversations unfolded, both of you spoke about how things might have gone differently, more positively. And you both have expressed willingness to actively engage with the other's wish to connect. You both have expressed wishes to clarify confusions and misunderstandings and to understand differences. You have both slowed down enough to expose your need for each other. Rather than focusing on blaming each other for shortcomings, you each have been able to entertain alternative interpretations of how and why conversations have gone amiss. This has helped you to see eye to eye more often. That's the pattern we've been trying to develop. And I am witness to the fact that this pattern exists between you at times. I have seen you respond to each other in this way."

"I'm glad to hear something is going right," Jim said.

Carole smiled.

This was perhaps the first moment of lightness they had shared with me. I pointed this out. "As we work together, we are going to address grievances you have with each other. But we will do that in a particular way. We will do that with a focus on trying to create emotional safety in the communication process. Emotional safety can be created by the way we talk about things; any conversation can be an opportunity to build emotional safety. *In fact, dealing with problems is often a supreme opportunity to build and repair connection.* That's how I'd like you to understand the healing process and the difficult conversations that are sometimes necessary."

Bringing the Third Dimension to Life

I also said, "When you speak, I would like to help you develop awareness of whether what you say to your partner is going to help create or detract from creating emotional safety. That's the third dimension of three-dimensional communication I've talked about with you. This awareness brings good energy to your core thoughts and feelings about the relationship. What are you doing that helps to build emotional safety in the relationship? Are you doing anything that tears it down? Are you open to learning how you can be more helpful to yourself and your partner in building emotional safety? If you study the relationship and understand ways in which your dedication to creating emotional safety can make a difference, that would be an act of love and devotion to each other. That's the kind of affirmation each of you needs in regular doses. It is the kind of devotion that sustains a loving relationship. You have many choices to make, and prime among them is this: In terms of an action plan, what would it mean if you were committed to creating emotional safety in your relationship? Is this something you want to do? If you work at this, the relationship has a vibrant chance to renew itself."

Neither responded to this statement, but they were listening, and it felt to me that they were listening *together*. There was so much about them I still didn't know, but, at least to this point, I had reason to feel encouraged about their ability to continue healing.

The tears and smiles they'd shared in sessions marked a softening, something they told me was not common for them. Each felt they had failed in their relationship with the other. Yet each also felt the other had failed them. Neither had come from a home where parents negotiated openly during emotionally charged disagreements. Neither felt confident or equipped to communicate about stressful topics. As a result, money discussions caused rancor, sex talks got skipped, and sharing ideas about parenting had been unproductive.

Although I have witnessed this juncture many times, I found Carole and Jim's arrival at this lonely place moving. I do not cry easily or often, but I felt tears form in my eyes at that moment they had joined in tears. Perhaps this was an expression of my own sense that the journey we embarked upon together would be daunting for me in some way as well as for them. Although I work with many couples, I confront my own feelings and learn things about myself as I go through this process. Perhaps something about them reminded me of a way in which I longed to be more able to open to myself or to my partner. Perhaps I viewed the apparent progress they were making in overcoming disconnection, or at least their coming to terms with understanding their situation, as similar to my own struggle to be a good partner and father. I felt this way, although my situation and theirs had some points of similarity as well as differences. Perhaps my tears symbolized my hope that throughout my work with them, I would stay emotionally present and help them learn not only a set of ideas about how to heal their relationship but to continue to open their hearts and feel from the inside what the other was going through. To help them do this, I needed to be open to my own feelings too. My tears reassured me that I was not speaking only from my head but that I was emotionally engaged as well. I thought, *Maybe this is a signal from me to myself that I was on the right track with them.*

Analyzing a Thin Slice of Behavior-Trying

Jim had opened the session by stating that he and Carole were having trouble talking to each other and needed to do more of it. Instead of validating his perception and the concern behind it, Carole had countered by stating that Jim could talk about talking, but he wasn't able to do it when it counted. She discredited his statement and in so doing demeaned the effort he had put into *trying*.

We associate doing with achieving. Changing behaviors means *doing* things differently. Trying to do, by comparison, can seem anemic. Often mere *trying* is offered up as an excuse for not achieving. And sometimes not achieving is a result of not trying hard enough.

Nonetheless, you can't expect to achieve changes without trying. And the change you desire often does not come on the first try. Nor on the second or third! Change takes persistence. Trying can be hard to track because it is so often invisible. Without success to show that the effort has been made, it can seem as if nothing was attempted. Yet trying has its own legitimacy and, in the end, is an indispensable element in the communication process. Genuine effort needs to be validated. It is not an excuse for not achieving but often a sign that change is on the way.

When a couples' communication pattern is stressful, signals are often misread or reversed. Think of a dyslexic student trying twice as hard as classmates to sound out syllables and getting nowhere while those around her complain that she isn't trying hard enough. Trying often entails an internal shift. Often it is a mental act, a behavior that cannot be duly observed but, nonetheless, is necessary for the transition from what-I-used-to-do in a specific situation to a what-I-do-now-that-works-better, a revised strategy or changed behavior. Carrying the analogy between the dyslexic student and the partner who is trying to change further, the student says, "I often misread a *b* for a *d*; how can I check myself to see if I'm doing that here?" And the point of finely attuned instruction is to help that student develop strategies to allow her to check and experience success where she has previously experienced only confusion, failure, and helplessness. For example, for the partner who becomes angry too quickly and who under such conditions tends to regret what ensues, this style of handling anger can be understood as a mistake that needs correcting. It can be seen as a habit that can be unlearned or replaced rather than as a genetic trait that cannot be altered. The process involved in regulating a bad temper is not easy, but, with determination, changes occur and progress can be achieved.

When asked how that distance between the old unsuccessful pattern and the newer improved one was achieved, the student who overcame her riotous confusion often says, "I learned a method. I made an effort. I tried. And then I was able to do *it.*" And applied to couples work, that "it" could stand for anything from gaining better control over a temper to identifying a feeling to resisting the habit of criticizing in favor of listening patiently and then considering what response would most likely further build emotional safety.

Trying involves learning just as learning involves trying. Partners need to encourage each other's efforts *to try to learn.* An atmosphere of reproach is not conducive to either trying or learning.

As much as speaking and respecting emotions, learning is key to relational healing. Do you find that surprising? Many people do. Of course, much of that learning centers on learning about feelings and about the similarities and differences in your ways of seeing and doing things, including how you and your partner each process your thoughts and emotions.

Mistake Magic

When you try to do what you don't yet know how to do, you inevitably make mistakes. Mistakes are often associated with destructive blunders. But they are part of almost all learning processes. The culture of a good relationship must support certain types of mistakes, especially those that lead to new understanding. For example, as a partner learns to identify and articulate her feelings, she may make errors in how and when to express them. That's to be expected. Even tolerated. Sometimes celebrated.

Intentionality (or Lack Of)

The things we say to one another, each verbal communication, has many different facets. We link up with the facet that we are most interested in, the one we are looking to find or understand most readily.

For example, when Jim said, "We're here because we don't seem to be able to talk to each other without fighting." Instead of validating his concern as important, Carole criticized him for "sounding" like he was interested in working on the relationship when he spoke, but then failing to follow through. Carole might have taken the opportunity to join with him. She could have validated his statement as a perceptive one. She might have said she agreed and asked in a friendly and inviting way how they could build on their agreement as allies to work together to change things. That was one possible facet (or interpretation) of Jim's message that Carole might have used as an opportunity for connection. She might have validated it in a spirit of cooperation. But her *intention* was to do otherwise. She listened with her antenna trained on finding the facet that she actually did develop. Rather than confirm a point of commonality, she interpreted his statement—a statement she agreed with—as a misrepresentation of the way Jim was functioning in their relationship. She took his statement as an opportunity to introduce a different train of thought—the idea that he may *sound* like he is thoughtful and expressive about the relationship but that this only *seems* like it's true. In actuality, she claimed he is good at "talking the talk" but does not follow through and said that it leaves her feeling alone and hurt much of the time.

Food for thought: Carole hears Jim say one thing, and instead of embracing it because she agrees with it, she debunks it because she feels he doesn't live up to what he says he thinks he should be doing. Her criticism has the effect of alienating him from the issue. Is this a step in the direction of emotional safety? Or a step away? (See Appendix 4 for my response.)

Why does Carole criticize Jim in this instance? What's in it for her? She could have responded to his statement in a way that promoted a feeling that they were approaching a common vision of the work that needed to be done. Instead she criticized him and undermined his credibility. She reasserted distance between them, pushed him away. The benefit to her is only as a defensive maneuver.

Basic trust between Carole and Jim needed to be rebuilt. Each had developed negative expectations of the other's ability or intention to support and cherish each other.

As we began our work, none of the reasons for her remaining steadfastly defensive have any bearing on judging her as either a good or bad person. I came to believe that the reasons she acted as she did pointed to her being unhappy. By the way, Jim did the same thing when he jumped from a moment of tearful and emotionally intimate connection to a disdainful comment about how unsurprising Carole's expression of pain and blame had been to him. Instead of validating her pain and sharing concern about it, he swerved into a negative direction with his dismissive comment. This does not mean he is a contemptuous *person*. It means that he was feeling defensive and used contempt to mask his fear of being hurt or disappointed again. Each partner is averse to feeling helpless or disempowered. Defense is often motivated by the need to fend off feelings of helplessness and vulnerability but at the expense of openness to connection. After all, defensiveness marshals the power to repel or reject the approach of the other. This is genuinely self-protecting if the other is attacking, but not when they are making a bid for connection.

Negativity

How is it that Jim and Carole had become so stuck in this pattern, like many other couples? It was because they tried to use the force of anger and accusation in their struggle against negativity, and, emotionally speaking, two negatives do not make a positive. They were unable to *harness the desire for connection* that was embedded within their anger. They were unaware of how to do that. The force of connection could, and eventually did, provide the breakthrough energy they needed. They had not understood it was there for them. That it actually was accessible. Yet it was. This method of three-dimensional communication eventually enabled them to understand and utilize that energy to create emotional safety.

Rebuilding the damaged foundation of a house of love cannot be accomplished solely by an exacting analysis of the damage done. Understanding the cause of the damage is important to safeguarding against re-creating it. But simply knowing what went wrong does not necessarily yield knowledge of how to make it right. To make it right, emotional safety must be integral to the new design.

Beyond that, preoccupation with the negative can distract partners from creating what they need: reasons to trust and reasons to feel safe and loved.

The rebuilding process must provide partners with good reasons to feel that it makes sense to keep trying to make things work. In this regard, nothing galvanizes success like success. Carole began to trust Jim when she felt that he was through being contemptuous, when he began validating her feelings and perspective. She needed to *feel* that before she could begin to allow herself to renew trust in him. Likewise, Jim needed to feel that Carole would come through for him in similar ways.

EXERCISE IN HOPE

Do you have a sense of how you contribute to a mood of openness in your relationship? Can you identify ways in which you contribute to a mood of unfriendliness in your relationship?

You may or may not agree with the ways in which your partner complains about aspects of the relationship. Nonetheless, do you reserve a place within yourself to think about how it feels for her to feel the way she does?

Do you have a way of thinking about your partner's perspective that neither passes judgment nor defends against the "rightness" or "wrongness" of what she feels?

Do you understand how your partner's feelings make sense to her? If so, you are on your way to a more empathic relationship. If not, we have identified a key defect in your communication process. Without empathy and deep understanding, sustaining love in your relationship will not be possible. If this is a problem for you, you can make headway by working on it.

Take a few minutes and jot down your thoughts about this. Make it your goal to describe your partner's complaints clearly, as if you sympathized with her, whether or not you do.

Paint yourself a picture in words (or shapes if you like to draw!) of your partner's fondest hopes for an improved relationship between you and her. Having this picture can be extremely beneficial for both of you.

Also, think of your vision of your relationship at its most hopeful and evolved. Describe that situation in as much detail as possible. Both of these visions will be beneficial as you develop your three-dimensional communication skills and grapple with what creating emotional safety involves. It most certainly will involve an understanding of each other's fondest hopes for the future!

How can we develop a new way of communicating, one that features opening up rather than shutting down? Sometimes something small, even a smile, can be a catalyst in taking you and your partner forward. But it's not as simple as being able to smile together. In addition to the smile, you need acknowledgments and appreciation that support the connection and the wish to strengthen it. After all, within a loving smile lies a meaning that can drive and deepen love. Awareness of its meaning brings the third dimension into focus and validates its power.

Part Two

Recovering
a Relationship

CHAPTER FIVE

Diane and Jaime on the Bridge

Let your hopes, not your hurts,
shape your future.

—Robert H. Schuller

Diane and Jaime walked arm in arm past the array of bistros and specialty cafés. Her pudding-bowl pageboy gave her otherwise worried expression an ironic twist. Somebody might have thought she was too cute to have so many worries. Jaime knew better. His hair was short on the sides and somewhat longer on the top. The couple pushed south on the winding street, pavement glistening from the earlier sun shower.

The May evening was unseasonably warm and muggy. Both were exhausted. Jaime pushed to keep up with Diane. He had come directly from a five-hour session in the digital lab. He was poised to complete the MFA program at the New School in photography. He also carried a concentration in journalism. He was the first in his large Italian-American family to receive a college degree, and, although he was proud of the accomplishment, he now felt at a distance from the brothers, sisters, and parents with whom he still identified closely.

Now forty, Jaime had spent over fifteen years in the advertising industry. Paired with a graphic designer, he had gone from being a novice to a trusted old hand. He had made his way from copy-writing, editing, and directing to producing successful TV spots. His two-person team had become known for clever copy and arresting images. They had garnered industry awards and financial perks, but unrelenting pressure to top former accomplishments left Jaime feeling depleted and hungry for something different. The discontent led him to graduate school.

After graduation, he was determined not to slip into having his schedule controlled by market research or corporate strategists. He wanted something else. A friend had asked what that "something else" might be. All he could say was, "That's what I'm trying to figure out." As he approached completion of the last semester of his master's program, he had come no closer to knowing what he was going to do next.

Sober for the last four years, Jaime credited the Twelve-Step program with having helped him to do "what I couldn't have done by myself." He followed the program devotedly, except in one regard: he had gotten involved with Diane before completing his first year of sobriety. In all other ways, he endorsed and followed program recommendations faithfully.

As he approached graduation, a well-established glossy magazine with important ties to online and media outlets offered Jaime a staff position that promised good pay and security. Diane was thrilled. Jaime was wary.

He anticipated that jumping directly into another full-time position with assured overtime demands would make him feel like school had been only a footnote between jobs. What he hoped to experience in his career was a dramatic turning point. He was looking to feel himself build momentum and take off professionally. He had felt this way in the early days of his work in advertising, and he wanted to reexperience that excitement elsewhere. Work at the magazine felt to him like settling.

He and Diane had separate apartments but had been living more together than separately over the past three years. If they were to move in together, it would be important that he have a steady income. For this reason, he considered the offer carefully, albeit unenthusiastically.

The couple strolled down Clinton to Delancey Street in lower Manhattan. There they crossed to the other side of the broad east-west thoroughfare and turned left, entering the walkway of the Williamsburg Bridge that linked Manhattan with Brooklyn.

As they ascended the walkway, the skyline glittered behind them.

"I can't believe you are even considering letting this opportunity go," Diane said.

Diane was a choreographer. Whereas Jaime was a native New Yorker, Diane had been drawn to the city by opportunity and the allure of stardom. She had experienced exciting successes, but had not been able to discontinue her "day" job. She was a night-shift cocktail waitress at a downtown music club. The tips were exceptional and the job offered enough flexibility to allow her to audition and pick up occasional freelance work, but at thirty-three she felt marginal to her chosen profession and far behind the timetable she had hoped to maintain. She despaired about her future in the dance world. The series of professional accomplishments she had experienced had at times been inspiring but felt disjointed. Where were they leading? Like a kaleidoscope of images joined only by the sequence of their appearance, the pattern failed to form connecting dots that could be identified as a career path. Her professional support network was a hodgepodge of talented but struggling artists, all straining to keep a hand in their creative work. Whenever the chance for dance work came her way, once again she felt that she was starting from scratch. In addition, she hoped to become a mother but felt despairing as to whether this would be in the cards for her.

The Critical Conversation

Diane turned to Jaime, a hint of scorn in her voice. "What's the point? Do you have to pound the pavement for a year or two, wishing and hoping for an opportunity like this to come along before you are ready for it? Chances like this don't come every day. I can guarantee you that this is a great, maybe a once in a lifetime, opportunity. Do you realize that?"

Jaime walked beside her, his mouth tight. He let go of her hand and his arm swung between them. As far as he was concerned, they had been down this conversational road before. And from his point of view it had not been pleasant or productive.

If she could have read his thoughts she would have heard something like *Have you been listening to anything I've been saying? Yes, it's a good opportunity. I know that. But the opportunity presented itself because I am really good at what I do. Other opportunities will present themselves. I know that you have been working at the music club for way too long and that the idea of letting something like this pass feels crazy to you. I get that. But I'm not you. I understand how and why it would make sense for you to go out for a comparable opportunity in your field. But I'm in a different place with it. I want you to see this from my point of view, and not simply try to stuff the way you think about it into me.*

As they approached the center of the span, the light on the water shone silver. A bluesy saxophone could be heard off in the distance. A light breeze wafted slender notes high above the East River. The subway bound for Brooklyn clattered past, a cacophony of metallic groans.

Diane tried to catch Jaime's eye, but he was fixed on something that kept her outside his gaze. This is what Jaime looked like when he was triggered, before his anger flared.

"What do you think about what I'm saying?" she said.

"I think I'm fed up hearing about what you think about this. I don't need it and I don't want it. Why don't you turn around and go back to the apartment. I need to walk on by myself."

Diane froze like a mute silhouette against the high arc of the bridge. She only vaguely apprehended her own thoughts, the ones she wished she could gather.

Jaime tramped on through puddles of moonlight. Like a runaway locomotive, he accelerated steadily, without a conscious thought as to where he'd end up.

He had been on this side, the runaway side, of arguments and conversations with girlfriends before, but not with Diane.

While she could still see him, she called out, "Jaime, don't do this. I can't take this. Don't do this to me."

He did not turn around but only shifted his head to the side. From afar she heard his muffled reply, "But you know how to dish it out. You did it to yourself. You don't listen."

"Jaime, don't go. We can talk about it." Between the long-gone clack of the gray-black train and the falling-down horn lines, Diane tasted her tears.

"Good-bye, Diane." His words rode a backdraft and reached her like the muted echo of an echo.

She was no longer listening; she was remembering. Her eyes reddened more deeply with every breath.

Jaime walked for a long time that night and resolved to shut Diane out of his good graces. Eventually his anger softened. The next day when he approached her, their conversation resulted in another abrupt leave-taking. This time she was the one who said "Good-bye."

♥ ♥ ♥

The night before I first met Jaime, he had gotten through to Diane on the phone. He reported saying, "I'd really like to talk about what happened. Can't we talk this over?"

She replied, "I asked you that question the other night. You gave me your answer. It was no. Let's stick with it. Besides, we don't know how to talk anything over. That's been proven. I'm not going to give you another chance to tear me down." She paused before continuing. "I've got to go. I can't talk about this now." And she was gone, as fast and faraway as his footsteps had been on the bridge.

In the aloneness after she hung up, he felt enclosed in shadow, entangled in wisps of guilt and shame. But also he sensed a coolness, a quiet. He collected himself in the slowed-down moment. Nothing was going to happen in the stillness, not right then anyway, so he took some time and began to reason. *Diane was right about a lot of what she was saying. You can't shut somebody out and then turn around and expect them to open up to you.* He understood that no one could do that. And Diane shouldn't have to. He was thinking that he had not been fair to her. So why should she trust him? He'd have to give her a good reason to trust, and right now she didn't have any.

He told me that he and Diane had planned on moving in together after he graduated, and that he had not expected the relationship to end when it did. "I want to get back with her, but I don't know if that's realistic," he said.

Before leaving his apartment to come to my office, he'd looked around his living room without knowing what he was looking for. Then it had come to him. He was looking for some sign that she was still there. Something to indicate that what had happened had been an illusion and that somehow things were back to the way they had been. He was looking for a sign that it wasn't really over. Eyes moist, he turned away and begrudgingly locked the door and walked on.

"I want to show her that I can do better than what I've done." He spoke emphatically but without making eye contact with me. It was as if he was trying to persuade someone, some onlooker who knew better than to take his word at face value, that he was going to follow through with what he was saying. "Even though it's only been a couple of weeks, I feel like I've learned a lot. I can do things differently now because I understand things differently now."

I questioned him about what those different "things" were, those different understandings. He described situations in which he felt he would have been better off holding his temper than giving in to it. He told me the story of the conversation they'd had on the bridge. "It could have gone very differently."

"In what way?" I said.

"I didn't have to lose my temper like that."

The Problem with Making Anger the Problem

Many couples feel that what is wrong with their communication process is that it fails to prevent conflict and anger. But conflict and anger are inevitable. Many couples complain, "We fight too much. Most everything else in our relationship is okay, except we can't seem to avoid conflict. And once we are angry at each other, it takes a lot for the mood to pass."

Studies indicate a contradictory picture. Researchers find that partners who argue regularly are no better or worse than couples who rarely do. Key findings underscore that what counts most is whether partners know how to resolve their conflicts without damaging trust.

That's not to say that knowing how to fight or argue without damaging trust is the key, either. Old school couples therapists often engaged couples in training them to "fight fair," so that they would control the damage done when they argued or disagreed. There is nothing wrong with learning techniques to limit destructive conversation, but what saves the couples that take conflict in stride is something different. It is making regular contributions to a reservoir of trust that becomes the foundation of their relationship. That is what makes conflict safer.

How Do You Measure Trust?

Trust is not generally measured by intensity, but it has to be deep-rooted enough to withstand the intensity of strong emotion when stress is high. Rather than being intense, a sense of unshakable connection—trust—must be fundamental. The third dimension generates this kind of fundamental connectedness.

Diane and Jaime did not have a fundamental trust-strengthening process safeguarding their connection. Neither knew how to form or practice it. Both felt helpless and sometimes hopeless in the face of conflict. This fundamental deficiency set the stage for Diane and Jaime's bond to fray, weaken, and eventually sever.

Three-dimensional communication inoculates partners against finding themselves defenseless in the face of disagreement. In my first book, *The Power of the Middle Ground*, I write about couples' ability to strengthen and maintain an emotional autoimmune system; three-dimensional communication is a variation on this theme. When things get tough, you need to have something tough going for you. Three-dimensional communication can be characterized as a gentle process because it involves reflection and, at times, restraint. But resilience is the fruit of that gentleness. It takes root from down-to-earth acceptance, here-and-now engagement with the unchangeable facts of the moment, combined with dedicated focus on making the most of the moment's possibilities.

Let's consider a hypothetical follow-up conversation between Diane and Jaime to illustrate how having a three-dimensional perspective might have changed the outcome of their evening.

Listening Is Not a Neutral Act

As the couple began climbing onto the bridge, Diane had said, "I can't believe that you are even considering letting this opportunity go."

Diane's comment conveyed harshness and a lack of curiosity or respect for what is going on within Jaime. A downward spiral had been set into motion.

This direction of the conversation was not solely derived from what Diane said. Jaime's *interpretation* of her words pushed it further toward disconnection. He had felt that she had shown disdain for him. This was his knee-jerk reaction. It is understandable he might feel this way, but, if we are going to think about three-dimensional communication here, we need to entertain other possible directions he might have gone in response to her words.

Rather than thinking in terms of how her words had disparaged him, what if he had set out to understand what her words said about *her* view of *her* situation? He might have gone in *that* direction. Rather than assuming she was judging him or positioning herself as the more insightful of the two, he might have considered her remark as some kind of signal that she was feeling distress within herself. He might have construed it as a means of calling attention to feeling alarmed, at not being able to feel secure in her connection with him.

If Jaime had asked himself, "What do her statements mean in terms of her sense of *our* connection?" it might have diverted the conversation from arriving at the mutually alienating place that it finally reached. Seeing something three-dimensionally gives the viewer an opportunity to reset their vantage point. Shifting perspective often uncovers previously unnoticeable aspects of a complex reality. As a result, the importance of initially obscure elements can be brought into focus. New meanings and new possibilities for understanding and connection can and do emerge. When analyzed in depth, sometimes what feels like contempt to the listener is a signal of the speaker's insecurity; it has precious little to do with haughtiness or disdain and everything to do with a frustrated desire for secure attachment.

Instead of revving up to withdraw from Diane because of her perceived unfriendliness, he might have wondered, "What does her statement say about how she feels about her place in the relationship?" Asked in an openhearted spirit, this question links Jaime to the third dimension of his dialogue with Diane. The question brings emotional safety from the margin to the center of concern.

As it unfolded, Jaime had received the message in the way in which he understood it to have been delivered: without a trace of curiosity or compassion. We know what resulted. In the original conversation, neither partner moved the talk toward a meeting of minds or hearts. Neither partner layered in explicit concern for emotional safety. In this sense, they abandoned each other.

How You Open Is How You Close

I am analyzing the opening of the dialogue as closely as possible because research indicates that dialogues between couples hinge on the tone with which they begin. Dialogues that begin poorly tend to end that way. Unless either Diane or Jaime had rallied with something extraordinary, this conversation was effectively doomed from the start. Conversations need to be front-loaded with encouragement, clarity, support, and *positive intention.*

If you, as so many of us do, routinely bypass this internal step in the communication process—the step in which you reflect on whether what you are saying or hearing contributes to building emotional safety—you leave yourself wide open to miscommunication and disconnection. Strive to weave this heightened awareness of emotional safety into your dialogue. It creates goodwill. It mitigates relational damage. It keeps disagreements in perspective.

I discussed with a colleague the situation Jaime had described to me. My colleague said, "When Jaime received Diane's harsh message, he had a choice about how to respond." My colleague emphasized that if Jaime had extended goodwill and trust to Diane, this might have stemmed his anger, relaxed the mood, and given them a chance to see eye to eye. This kind of internal shift, internal flexibility, is an important aspect of what it takes to create emotional safety.

About Choices

Although I agree with my colleague's observation, I also believe that the choice Jaime had was meaningful only to the extent that he was in the habit of making choices about his responses. If he is in the habit of reacting without thinking, then he really has no choice. He's stuck with the behavior that emerges without his conscious input. The third dimension introduces real choice and, therefore, real freedom into a couple's dialogue.

If Jaime were already practicing three-dimensional communication at the time he was on the bridge with Diane, he might have considered her initial remark as my colleague suggested. This would have been a *possibility*. In this respect, three-dimensional communication generates possibilities. Someone asked me angrily, "What is the third dimension, some kind of magic? The possibilities exist within it but not elsewhere? This sounds like psychobabble, gobbledygook."

I responded, "The possibilities are always there. There are always numerous options to follow in dealing with a complex situation. Thinking three-dimensionally helps you to see what those options are. Is a telescope magic because it pulls into view an object that is too distant to be seen with the naked, unfocused eye? Does the telescope create the object in the distance? Of course not. Neither does three-dimensional thinking create options. It allows us to see them, though. It is a tool. We can use it if we know how it works."

Change Generates Worry

For many couples, change generates worry about whether the relationship can tolerate the stress of a transition. Transitions, even positive ones, can provoke disorientation. They disrupt the security of familiar routines. The familiarity of routine often brings comfort. I learned later that Diane had seen the possibility of Jaime working at the magazine as a safe haven for their life together. Because Jaime was graduating, some form of change was inevitable. Rather than trying to take over his thought process and force him to bow to the strength of her ideas, she felt she was making a gallant attempt to defend the future of their relationship by urging him to take the job. For her it represented a way out from having to endure the anxiety that uncertainty about his future employment and their finances would bring. If Jaime had entertained the idea that Diane felt that their relationship itself might be in jeopardy if he didn't take this job, he might have validated her concerns and perhaps even offered some reassurance, a vote of confidence in their future—with or without that particular job situation.

If Jaime had been able to suspend his critical perspective as they talked, perhaps he would have been able to hold off focusing on what she was doing to him, and he might have arrived at appreciating this question: "If she is trying to be helpful, how is it that what she said came across as hostility?" Often, when you analyze the deeper levels of relationship, you find that much anger is caused by frustrated desires to locate a sense of security in the relationship situation. That frustration can and does trigger feelings of desperation, helplessness, and hopelessness and can often be misread as belligerence.

Looking to blame or justify anger, partners often miss the meaning of remarks that are designed—sometimes clumsily—to forge connection. We tend to see what we are looking for, what we are expecting to see. Unfortunately, while on the lookout for what we expect to find, we narrow our scope and can overlook valuable information that is not within the parameters of what we expect to see. It is easy to expect things to be as they have been and thus miss opportunities to notice a partner's willingness to do things differently than anticipated.

Consider what might have followed if Jaime had said, "You know, honey, we are both going through a lot right now. I understand that you have strong feelings about whether I should take this job or not. I also understand that we don't see eye to eye on this. We can talk about it more. And we will. But I want to tell you that I'm confident we are going to get through this thing okay. As a couple, we are going to be fine. I'm going to be there for you, and I need you to be there for me. That's most important. Let's not let the tension of these changes pull us apart. We need each other more than ever now. I want our relationship to work out because I love you."

Which Part of You Has the Floor?

This short speech Jaime might have said *represents how Jaime felt.* You may rightly wonder, "How is it that while in the moment he didn't say anything like this?" That's because Jaime is a complicated person, as we all are, and the part of him that was in control overruled the part of him that might have made the statement above. Nonetheless, those feelings, as future interactions make clear, do reflect a part of what Jaime was feeling.

The problem is that he was not in that moment sufficiently connected to this part of himself; let's call it his most loving part. Have you ever heard the expression that a person is "out of touch" with him- or herself? This is a good illustration of how and why this is an important idea.

Why was he out of touch? Because he was not in the *habit* of responding with that part of himself, the part dedicated to creating emotional safety. Another way of understanding it is to say that he had not integrated this part into his dialogue with Diane. This is the same thing as saying that they had not developed a three-dimensional connection. Defensiveness and anger *obscured* these deeper feelings. Responding three-dimensionally involves responding with a part of yourself that is always present as a potentiality but often remains unvoiced, undeveloped, and underutilized.

In the course of our work together, Jaime remarked, "In a sense, I betrayed myself by not representing that part of myself. Instead, the hothead part took over. The part that had the long-range view of what I need got shunted to the side. This has caused me a lot of pain. It's also done a gross disservice to my relationship."

I'm calling that the angry part, and most of us have such a part, the reactive part; it is the part that responds without thinking, the part that acts on autopilot.

Jaime continued. "What I actually did, the way I handled myself, left what was in my best interests out of the picture. I hurt myself and I hurt my relationship. I want to learn how not to do that going forward."

This was the work we had cut out for us. I told him that I would help him to do that. I told him that we had already begun doing that when discussing these ideas. But we both knew that the ideas alone would not be sufficient to bring about the changes Jaime was looking for. The trick was to bring the ideas and ways of handling thoughts and feelings into a practice that was available to him in real time, especially when he was in difficult or stressful conversations. The goal is to develop ongoing awareness of what constitutes mindfulness, long-range perspective, compassion, and emotional safety.

♥ ♥ ♥

So far we have discussed a few ways the conversation on the bridge might have been prevented from flowing toward hard feelings and disconnection. Diane might have substituted a less accusatory, less harsh statement. Hearing what she said, Jaime might have considered it from a different perspective than the one he adopted. He might have "taken it differently" is the colloquial way to say that. And that "different" way would have been one that was more compassionate toward himself and Diane. Employing three-dimensional communication, then, involves listening and speaking with compassion in such a way that the intent to do so shines through.

Makeover Talk

Let's now consider what might have happened had Diane opened the dialogue with this statement instead of the abrasive statement she actually made: "I'm trying to put myself in your place and understand what your thoughts are in considering this job."

As I have come to know him, Jaime would not have been triggered by this toned-down remark. Had Diane offered this alternate statement, she would have validated thoughtfulness as a primary element that she was seeking to activate in their dialogue. What are the characteristics of this alternate statement? It is empathetic, not judgmental.

When she articulates the idea that she views putting herself in his place to understand how he is thinking about things—the definition of empathy—she is implicitly validating that he is worth thinking about, of interest, and that his thoughts and feelings are of value. These messages are subtle and, even in a three-dimensional dialogue, are rarely articulated directly. Instead they become part of the very atmosphere of three-dimensional conversation. And they have enormous power. These messages are felt. They create the underpinning of emotional safety for speaker and listener. They create the richness that characterizes an intimate connection, the essence of delicious closeness that partners sense when able to speak about difficult topics without threatening each other.

This second, empathic statement Diane makes, the makeover, is a far cry from her initial (harsh) statement in its implications. But is it more difficult to come up with the language that fosters three-dimensional connection than to speak the other way? I think you will agree that it is not. Difficulty doesn't enter into it. What's involved is breaking one habit and replacing it with another. Dialogue layered with curiosity, respect, and openness involves intentionality above all else. Dialogue that is populated with moments in which emotional safety is created and strengthened emerges from this. The old way of speaking on autopilot without considering emotional safety withers away through the practice of intentionally creating this reservoir of trust that we all need and crave.

If Jaime had intuited that Diane was feeling insecure about their relationship, the events on the bridge would have been quite different. Either partner could have helped to slow down the back-and-forth dialogue and at the same time enriched their sense of connection. At the time, though, neither was tending the connection and, perhaps unknowingly, both mutilated it.

Had Jaime been able to generate conscious concern for what was happening to their bond during their talk, he probably would not have looked away as he did when he began to get triggered. Then he would probably have noticed that Diane was looking for him, trying to make eye contact. Perhaps he could have reassured her then and there, and as soon as the noisy train passed they would have turned toward each other and hugged. Standing there, suspended over the dark waters with unseen stars above, feeling like a couple and relieved of momentary tension, perhaps they would have kissed in the night shadow and then walked home in a shared silence back toward Delancey Street. Under these circumstances, what if they looked back on their conversation and each separately thought and felt that they were finding a way forward together?

Not only the things that get talked about but the *way* things get talked about makes for outcomes that are worlds apart, which include not just new ways of talking but new *dimensions* of understanding. Their first talk, the breakup conversation, never got near what we are calling our third dimension. The reimagined talk started and stayed there. Communication is not about words spoken but understandings created. We slow down reactivity to intensify connection; the slow-down is the shortcut to contact. Given that the first destructive conversation actually happened, let's follow Jaime and Diane forward in the next chapter to see how three-dimensional communication can be applied for the purpose of healing deep damage already suffered.

CHAPTER SIX

I Can't Read Your Mind, but I Need to Know Your Heart

In Asian languages, the word for mind and the word for heart are the same. So if you're not hearing mindfulness in some deep way as heartfulness, you're not really understanding it.

—Jon Kabat-Zinn

It was autumn by the time Diane came to see me. Jaime and I had gotten together for individual sessions during the summer. He was hoping she would eventually join us, while at the same time preparing himself for the possibility that she would not. Diane had told Jaime she needed time to think about what she wanted. For nine weeks they had no contact. Then in mid-September she called and set up an appointment to see me.

I had already gotten to know Jaime somewhat. If Diane felt I was more aligned with him than with her, couples work would be compromised. For this reason, I aimed to balance the number of individual sessions I had with each over the course of whatever work we did together. Getting to know her and conveying that understanding to her was crucial. I proposed seeing Diane without Jaime before seeing them together.

In the early phase of work, many partners feel pessimistic about whether couples therapy can help them. This stems in part because couples tend to wait too long before coming in for couples work. Research tells us that couples average a whopping six years from the time they identify a serious problem in their relationship to the time they come in to try to deal with it. By then it is not unusual for resignation to have set in. This pessimism at the beginning of couples work also comes from being unable to distinguish between aggravated difficulties that doom the renewal of a couple's communication, and a situation in which marked improvement can come about relatively quickly if both partners commit themselves to learning and practicing basic communication skills. For those in the latter category, learning to connect empathically, or at least not to crash helter-skelter into each other's hopes and dreams, can evoke the breath of inspiration. Because expectations for a breakthrough had been so low, techniques that facilitate garden-variety reconnection can feel like a throw-away-the-crutches revival experience. For those in the former category, whose difficulties are advanced and entrenched, the road back is harder. Oftentimes, these couples can be helped to return to contemplate the roots of how and why they were first attracted to each other. From there, an analysis of the issues that derailed them can rekindle hope. If destructive patterns such as blaming, belligerence, and stereotyping can be identified and acknowledged, and partners can generate a heartfelt commitment to creating emotional safety together, negative patterns can be modified, worked through, and even eliminated—think crisis intervention and rejoining. With that accomplished, building a three-dimensional communication pattern can help them create a new beginning.

During that first session, Diane sat in the green leather recliner across from me and shifted side to side as she gathered herself. I could almost hear her thinking, *Where do I begin?* She peered down at a space halfway between us and then just as quickly looked away. Still gazing toward the window on my left, away from the chocolate-colored cloth of my upholstered seat, she spoke. "I am not sure if I can or want to reunite with Jaime. But understanding why the relationship ended the way it did would be helpful to me. For now, we can say that's why I'm here. And whatever he learns about himself in the process will be good too."

She lowered her voice to a scratchy whisper. "There is so much about Jaime I love. But, even though this may sound strange, I don't think he can understand what it is to be loved or to love. Not really." Her thin brows grew closer. "There is a part of him that always holds back and I think always will. I don't think he realizes it. It's just the way he is." Her coal-black eyes shifted focus, locking on to mine. "He can be loving but then withdraw and withhold. To me, his withholding has always been our biggest problem. He holds back even when he is giving. My need to feel loved doesn't come across; he doesn't get me. Maybe he doesn't feel special within himself. Whatever the reason . . . he doesn't make me feel special. And that's what I need."

The way she spat out "whatever the reason" indicated to me that she had given up on figuring out what his reasons might be; she had lost patience. Questions popped into my mind.

How much patience had she expended on Jaime before feeling depleted?

Had she ever experienced loving patience in any important relationship?

How much patience had her parents had with her?

What were her previous relationships like?

Had there been some way in which Jaime needed, and perhaps wanted and would have welcomed, Diane's help in establishing that she was very important to him?

This last question occurred to me because, as I'd gotten to know Jaime, it was clear to me that she was important to him. This was a point of disconnection. Part of my job would be to help them re-approach this issue with compassion for each other.

The questions I formulate early in my work with a couple help me to organize and personalize my approach. With that in mind, other questions occurred to me.

What did she mean when she said she didn't feel special to him?

Did she mean he was not prioritizing her in relation to other people or activities?

Did she mean that she felt he didn't carry her in his heart? That he did not think about her when they were apart?

What does she need to feel special? Does she know?

Was Jaime aware that Diane felt this way?

And if so, was he aware of what it meant to her to feel special?

Did he have any idea about what it would mean to move the rela-tionship in the direction of making her feel that way?

She continued. "We reached a tipping point, at least I did. Feelings of disappointment and loneliness reached a critical mass and made it impossible for me to believe we would ever get back to feeling relaxed with each other. It no longer surprised me when our conversations deteriorated into arguments that went nowhere and solved nothing. Once we hit that point, I felt pretty hopeless. Do you understand what I'm saying?"

"Yes, it sounds painful," I replied.

"It was," she said. "And it still is."

I thought, *She cited Jaime's withholding as key to their difficulties. Are there any issues of her own that she feels would need to be explored or resolved to improve the relationship? Does she have any faith in the possibility that Jaime could contribute to making things better?*

Expectations have a great impact on what partners are able or unable to accomplish in couples therapy. I wondered what her statements said about her deeper expectations in sitting with me.

Is she conveying doubts and fears to me as a way of signaling that she would not take any further emotional risks with Jaime?

Had she ever felt she could trust him more fully?

If so, what had happened? If not, did that have to do with his untrustworthiness, or did she have a history of difficulties in trusting people whom she felt close to, or to whom she wanted to feel close?

When had the trend of distrusting him, his ability to make changes, started?

Is it possible she feels too fragile to deal with or even acknowledge any need to modify her perspective or behavior as part of a healing process?

She said that she felt hopeless; did that mean that she had already exited the relationship and was using the work we were doing to make her exit more nuanced? Or was her expression of hopelessness a signal to me that she wanted help, wanted her hopes revived?

I leaned forward to hear her soft voice. "I don't mean that he needs to get me extravagant things, but he forgets anniversaries, he gets wrapped up in himself and doesn't follow through with making plans with me. I didn't feel I really mattered."

Diane told me that she did not believe that Jaime could or would be interested in changing. She seemed to view him as a person whose qualities were set. I wondered if she saw herself in the same light: fixed and unchangeable.

Sometimes while getting to know someone, you wonder about a perspective, knowing that it might turn out to be wrong. You consider it in order to rule it in or out. You may not understand how or why you know, or *think* you know, something about someone, but it turns out sometimes you eventually learn that your intuition is right. Sometimes, however, or at least this happens with me, you learn you've been off on a tangent so you reconfigure your approach. You must be willing to self-correct. That's true for me as a therapist, for sure. But it also is true for the partners. You've got to be active in thinking through the possibilities that are in front of you. Paying attention to marginal thoughts is an important aspect of the learning process, but as you explore the best routes for reconnection, you must be flexible. You have expectations, but being open to the possibility of experiencing surprises is a great advantage in doing healing work. Along these lines, more questions emerged.

Diane had experienced the interactions with Jaime as disappointing and depressing.

Had she carried a mood of despair into the relationship?

Had the breakup confirmed her expectation that good things were not in the cards for her?

Or had the breakup disrupted a confidence that had been growing in her life experience?

Had she met the challenge of failed communication between her and Jaime with energy and determination, or had she given up easily, fallen into a passive mode quickly?

My goal was to get to know her so that I had a handle on the answer to these questions. That would put me in a position to support her. Did she want me to support her in creating a new beginning with Jaime? Or was she looking to become liberated from feeling emotionally isolated in her relationship with him? Was she looking for me to support her in exiting the relationship? I owed it to her and to Jaime to approach these questions with as open a frame of reference as possible.

I explored these questions, considered them as hypotheses. I readied myself to inquire more deeply when I saw evidence that I was onto something relevant. I stood equally ready to abandon exploration that felt tangential. People reveal parts of who they are only when they are ready. Characteristics that seem clear at first can take on new and different meanings once understood in context. Case in point: In considering whether Diane was depressed before she met Jaime, I was trying to enlighten myself about whether or not Diane had possessed a reserve of good feeling about herself prior to the relationship with Jaime. Or had she entered the relationship feeling down and then had her hopes raised, only to be dashed? The relationship had opened a depressive trend for both partners. Both felt they'd been through a good deal of emotional distress. To what extent were there preexisting depressed feelings that surfaced and that could not be resolved within the relationship? To what extent was the relationship itself responsible for the emotional difficulties each partner faced?

My ability to make headway in exploring these questions would help Diane and Jaime undergo their own exploration of these issues. In all likelihood, any questions I asked of them they would be asking themselves. This was part of an overall strategy designed to help them to communicate their emotions to each other with more depth and accuracy.

Wanting to take nothing for granted, I explored a similar line of questions concerning Jaime.

Why did his anger flare so when he felt misunderstood by Diane?

How is it that he didn't seem to have confidence that he could help her to understand him more, along the lines he felt he needed to be understood, without having to get so angry?

How was anger discussed, conveyed, in his family when he was growing up?

Did he have any experience in his earlier life with adults speaking to one another about their feelings openly, tolerating disagreement, demonstrating patience and curiosity toward one another?

More generally, had he any experience of a role model for productive communication?

How secure was he in his sobriety?

Diane had voiced doubts about whether the kind of job opportunity he had been offered would come again anytime soon. Perhaps she had expressed doubts that he wished not to take seriously? Or which he felt without being aware he was feeling? Perhaps Diane's insistence that he could not afford to let this job opportunity pass him by triggered anxiety concerning his sense of assurance that there would be other offers should he change his mind. Had he gotten angry at her as a way of avoiding having to investigate his own feelings? Some of these questions would turn out to be useful, some not.

Diane and I were getting to know each other. Partners often hide their hopes, along with their hurts. They tend to "open up" when they feel supported and understood. Until then, hopes and hurts may be invisible but then surface in surprising ways.

I sympathized with the position she felt herself to be in. She had become alienated from Jaime. In spite of what she perceived as his shortcomings, she confided, "I am still attracted and attached to him. If I didn't feel that way, I don't think I could be here."

I empathized with her. I also felt Jaime's anguish at feeling unable to regain Diane's trust. Jaime said he would do whatever he needed to if he could get a second chance to work things out with her. In spite of what had gone wrong between them, he said, "When we connect, when things are going well, there is no one I would rather be with, no one I have ever been with who could make me feel as good. She is a fantastic person. I love her sense of humor, and, when we are not arguing, I appreciate her strong points of view about things, her ability to become passionately involved in projects. If I am not able to regain her trust, I will never be able to replace her, and it would take me a long time to get over the loss." Jaime convinced me that he had genuine warmth and love to share with Diane.

I asked him if he had shared these feelings with her when they were alone together. He replied, "I think so. I have told her that I care about her. I am not sure if I've told her exactly what I told you, though."

I encouraged him to let her know as fully as possible about these kinds of feelings. I asked him if he knew why it was that he might share certain of his feelings about Diane more openly with me than he had with her. He replied that he didn't know, but whatever the reason, it wasn't a good one. He told me he would spell out his feelings for her when he had the chance. "I am looking to do a lot of things better the second time around. I will make it harder for her to miss or mistake my feelings, from regrets to appreciation, if I can win back her trust."

When Confusion Abounds

Partners can be confused, not only about how their partner feels about them, but about how they themselves feel about their partner. When partners are unaware of how they feel, they are prone to act out feelings that are under the surface. When partners do things they later regret and cannot explain what their motivation had been, it is a sign that skills such as being able to identify, articulate, and regulate emotions need attention.

For many couples this is the most crucial phase of couples work. The development of emotional self-awareness—being able to identify how you feel—is a prerequisite for developing a three-dimensional bond.

Simple Miscommunication

Sometimes miscommunication really is about uncomplicated misunderstandings that, because they do not get corrected quickly, tend to make problems seem deeper than they are. Sometimes partners simply can't read each other accurately in the first dimension. Once they get their signals straight, they can feel relieved and reconnected. For most, the issues go beyond the first dimension, but the reason I mention this possibility is so that you have a sense that some couples need to appreciate how much they have going for themselves and take care not to overcomplicate how they approach the healing process. It was clear from the start that Diane and Jaime's problems went deeper than the first dimension.

Can You Read Your Partner?

When couples have trouble "reading" each other and then learn to do so, the next critical skill set that comes into play is their ability to trust each other. If beneath the confusion the partners have a well-developed ability to trust and integrate agreements and understandings, they are in good shape; however, if a breakthrough in the decoding of basic communication is accomplished and partners have difficulties with basic trust, in addition to basic communication, then the work goes forward with an emphasis on strengthening the third dimension of their communication. Rebuilding trust and creating emotional safety go hand in hand.

The view that men do a poor job of sharing warm and tender feelings with their partners is so common as to be a prevalent stereotype. About such men it is sometimes said, "It's hard to tell if he feels or what he feels. To believe he cares, you've got to take it on faith that he possesses some inner flame because, under normal circumstances, the most you'd ever glimpse of it would be a faint trace, a flickering shadow." Jaime is and was far from that type. More than most, he could be forthcoming and effusive. The more I got to know Diane, the more I understood that it was not a lack of affectionate or loving statements that triggered her complaints and doubts about Jaime. It was the way he worded and delivered what he said.

Your Heart May Be an Open Book, but That Doesn't Mean He Can Read Your Mind

Listen to a conversation that unfolded once the three of us had begun working together. Diane and Jaime had spoken about a number of difficult talks that felt unresolved, conversations that had gone poorly. I encouraged them to choose one of those conversations for us to work on. The idea would be to rediscuss it for the explicit purpose of creating emotional safety.

I prefaced the conversation. "As we talk about this, I'd like us to stay away from any concerns or comments about the correctness or incorrectness of either of your thoughts or feelings about the topic at hand. For this exercise, we need to let go of thinking in terms of right or wrong. What I would like you both to try to do is give each other a specific gift: the gift of feeling that you have been heard. That's what we're after. Listening without judging. Give yourself an internal directive: the point of what we are doing now is to convey understanding.

"Try to imagine the mind-set we are aiming for this way: It's the opposite of how we might listen if we were in a debate. In a debate, you prime yourself to use anything you hear to further your own point of view. You listen with an ear to *use what is said for your own purposes*. But here, try to listen with an ear toward your partner's need to feel heard. In a debate, you look for ways to persuade or convince. Here, you abandon that goal. In a debate, you pinpoint and expand on differences, real or implied. Here, we focus on points of connection, grounds for understanding. We look to validate the fact that thoughts and feelings have been successfully transmitted without utilizing the information received for any purpose other than as a confirmation of its content, and the fact that the content has been received.

"Again, I repeat for emphasis, we completely give over any attempt to convince or persuade. The reason I emphasize this so strongly is that, for most of us, listening competitively, debate style, is something we tend to do at times without even being aware we are doing it. So it takes intentionality to become aware of it to be able to monitor ourselves and control this tendency.

"In this exercise, you have a chance to create a space between yourselves in which each of you can feel safe to be who you are and say what you feel. You can disregard concerns about whether or not your partner agrees with you. The continuum of agreement or disagreement is not important now. You can feel secure in knowing that your partner has agreed that you have the right to feel whatever way you actually feel. We will explore feelings. Not whether the feelings are right or wrong, justified or not. The focus will be on awareness of feelings. Self-awareness and mutual awareness, those are the qualities we are nurturing.

"And you'll want to keep that third dimension mantra, 'Is what is happening contributing to or detracting from a sense of emotional safety in the relationship?' active in your thoughts. That's part of the intentionality that will help you both to resist any impulse to listen in that competitive or debate style.

"Opportunities to create emotional safety exist in virtually *any* conversation. Let's return to the one you've selected and see if we can find ways to do what we are setting out to do. Is this agreeable to you both?"

They nodded in agreement.

Jaime said, "Here is a conversation that ended in a huge blowup. After a certain point it turned into a shouting match. I hesitate to bring it up again, but I'm hoping that we will be able to discuss things like this differently going forward. That's my hope at least. Or at least that we will be able to talk about things like this without having it end up angry and unhappy. I know I said things that I regret and probably"—facing Diane—"you did as well. Anyhow, at some point in the conversation I said to Diane, 'You are the person I want to spend the rest of my life with. There is no one else but you. I have never cared for or loved anyone the way I love you.' Up to that point, the way I remember it, we were talking about various things and everything was going fine. What happened next?" Jaime asked Diane.

"Then I said, 'Do you want me to be the mother of your children?'"

"That's right. And then I said, 'Yes, I would like to have children with you. You know that. We've spoken about that.' That's how it began," said Jaime.

"Then I said, 'Then why don't you just come out and tell me that you want to have children with me? I feel like I have to beg you to say the things that I want to hear,'" Diane said.

Diane turned to me. "That's when things started getting angry. I saw Jaime tighten up and knew that we were heading downhill, but that was my authentic response to what he said."

Jaime shot back. "I didn't say anything about having children together because it wasn't the point I was making. I was trying to express to you how much I love you. I am completely mystified as to how we could get into an argument after a statement like that." Jaime placed the palm of his right hand across his forehead. He looked away from Diane and me and then positioned four fingertips and the tip of his right thumb against his brow. "If what I am trying to say doesn't match precisely what Diane wants to hear, she disregards what I am saying entirely. She points out the discrepancy between what I've said and what she wanted me to say. Her exclusive concern is the words she wants to hear as articulated within her thoughts. As if I could read her mind. And if I'm not able to produce those words, she feels I'm deliberately letting her down."

"Okay," I said. "Jaime, I get what you are saying about Diane being focused on what she wants to hear. But does your statement conform to your own inner concern: 'How can I move what we are talking about toward emotional safety?'"

"I'm not sure if it does or not. It is how I feel, though."

"It's how you feel and we are going to think about what you are saying, but remember that this is an exercise. And what I'm doing, the role I'm playing, is to slow you both down so you can stay with the directive: to reflect on whether the conversation is or is not creating emotional safety.

"As you've described it, you feel unheard when you believe Diane is not focused on what you say, but only on what she wants to hear. And that angered you and was part of what created a disconnection. Can you imagine some response in this situation other than a counterattack?" I paused. "You started out saying that you loved Diane, that you wanted to be with her forever. Diane, I have to say I was expecting that you might come back to Jaime with some kind of acknowledgment or appreciation of what he had said. You took the conversation in a different direction, though. Were you thinking about creating emotional safety when you asked Jaime about whether he wanted to have a child with you just then?"

Diane looked at me directly. "No. I wasn't thinking about emotional safety. I was thinking about the conversation we had and was repeating the way it had gone. I can see that I was not following the line of what Jaime was saying. I went somewhere else with it. I can see that I wasn't creating emotional safety, but I was putting a thought of mine out there, and I really wanted Jaime to respond to that thought."

"Okay," I said. "So you weren't thinking about emotional safety just then, and that reproduced the sequence as it happened the first time around. Let's keep going from there. Diane, I want to ask you: how does it feel to you, hearing Jaime say he believed that his words were not of interest to you unless they matched with what you had wanted him to say?"

"Well, I think that he's missing the point of what I was trying to say myself."

I replied, "Okay, I hear what you are saying, that he missed the point of what you had been trying to get across, but let's remember what this exercise is about. I'm trying to get you to respond to what he is feeling, not in terms of whether he is right or wrong to feel that way, but in terms of whether he can feel that you have really heard his feelings."

"I understand. I get that he feels I am not giving him a chance to be who he is and that makes him feel bad. That it eventually makes him feel angry."

"And does that make sense to you, if you consider it from his point of view?" I asked.

"Yes, I can see how he would feel that way."

Jaime spoke up. "These are the kinds of conversations, and we've had hundreds of them, that inevitably end in tears and accusations. And feelings of hopelessness for me."

He massaged his brow a moment before putting his hand down and continuing. "Once what I say is rejected—particularly if it is something that I would expect Diane to want to hear, like about how much I care about her—I get deflated at first. And then I get furious. It's like I've struggled to get myself to be as open and honest as I can be, and then I get disapproval for it. If I figure out and say what she wants to hear, I lose the chance to say what was on my mind in the first place. So I lose myself right there. If I do say what I want, with the words that feel like my voice, I lose Diane there. Either way, I feel defeated. And sometimes, even though I've tried not to, I explode and then regret what I say or do. But at those times, I feel like I don't have any other choice."

"Diane," I said, "how does it feel hearing that Jaime feels like he has no choice in situations like that?"

"I don't want him to feel that way. That's not a good way for him to be feeling in our relationship." She paused, looking intermittently at me and then away at the window. "The thing that he's missing is where I'm coming from in these conversations. When we have these kinds of conversations, I am almost always trying to work with myself to feel more connected, to feel safe and loved. He focuses on what I don't give him—like a feeling of approval or something. But I'm not trying to criticize him or make him feel bad. What I'm trying to do is steady myself. That's why I want to hear certain, very specific things because they will calm me down and let me know that he is hearing me, that we're connected, that he is able to locate me and grab me. It's ironic in a way that he thinks I'm trying to control him because what I'm trying to do is get him to help me find my own controls and help me get calmer. I am looking to hear the words that show me that he knows I'm lost and he is interested in helping me to feel found."

She turned to Jaime. "All I wanted was for you to say that you want me to be the mother of your children, that's what I needed to hear. I was feeling some kind of panicky feeling and those words would have made me feel like you knew and cared. I wanted to feel you weigh in against the panicky feeling I was trying to battle. I wanted to feel that you wanted to calm me. Sometimes I need you to be there for me in a very *specific* way. It's not that I don't want your way or your words. It's that I'm feeling pain, whether it makes sense for me to feel that way or not, and I want you to put a healing touch right where I feel the hurt. I want you to do the thing that I need you to do. Yes, I want to be the only one that counts in that moment because I want to know I matter to you. Maybe that's selfish, but I want to be able to be selfish sometimes. We're not talking right or wrong, right? I want to feel sometimes like you just forget about what's right or wrong and take care of me. I don't want to hear something that's close to what I need. I need to hear something that'll reassure me that you care enough to say exactly what I want you to say."

She stopped and closed her eyes for a moment. "And I want to feel that you won't take all this to be a burden but see it as something that you really want to do because you understand how much it means to me. And, in this case, if it was words about me becoming a mother, then that's what I needed. And maybe it's not even really about being a mother that's as important as me being in control of something. Not in control of you, though. It's not about me being in control of you. It's about me reinstating control within myself. If I could have heard you say those words, I would have felt better. Is that too much to ask? Is that so difficult? Am I being mean to you for wanting that?"

She faced me. "I don't understand why Jaime couldn't have simply said what I really wanted to hear. That's the part that gets to me. It's because what I'm asking for is simple and easy. And I know he can do it. Yet he doesn't. That's what I mean by withholding."

I responded first. "You've said a lot there. Jaime, does what Diane said make sense to you?"

Jaime looked at me and then to Diane. "Yes, I hear what you are saying. That you are not rejecting what I was saying, but that you wanted me to be your brakes and help you to slow down and feel safe. I get that. The thing is I want to talk about where this actually went when we spoke. The first time we spoke about it, we didn't get as far as we did today." Jaime squinted, and when he opened his eyes they were glistening. "I never said before that I understood she was not trying to overpower me. I never saw her as wanting me to join her. I didn't say it before because I didn't understand it that way before. I heard her say that today. I heard her better than I did before."

Diane said, "Well, that's a good thing."

"That is a good thing," I said. "That's an important thing." I made eye contact with both Diane and Jaime before continuing. "Jaime, did you feel that Diane grasped what you were saying? How did you feel when she said that she didn't want you to feel that you had no choice in these conversations?"

"I heard that. It made me feel good to hear that. And also that she was not trying to shut me down. That's an important thing for me to stay with. I think I've often felt that she didn't care about what I wanted to say, and what I was missing was that she had something she needed to say. And because she felt so much urgency, she couldn't listen. I don't know if I can always be patient enough to respond without feeling frustrated if I also have something I want to get across at the same time, but I do feel like this makes this conversation feel different, safer. Instead of feeling like we are attacking each other, it feels like the 'difficult' talks are really conversations in which either of us, or maybe both of us, is too stressed out to listen carefully. And when that happens we get into trouble."

I said, "Jaime, I think that's a great insight. When those conversations happen, the ones you described as often ending with hurt feelings and anger, they don't necessarily say anything at all about the way you feel about each other. But they say a lot about the way you are communicating at that time. Should you find yourself in a conversation like that again, you will hopefully notice two things: first, you are not slowing down the talk so that you can pay attention to how you are listening; and second, you are not giving yourself the space to ask the key question: Is what is happening now building or impairing emotional safety?"

CHAPTER SEVEN

Bridging the Impasse

The world is not comprehensible,
but it is embraceable: through the
embracing of one of its beings.

—Martin Buber

An Apology

Jaime leaned back in his chair. "There were times I lashed out. I felt cornered and didn't know what to do. I felt I was in a no-win situation. We've talked about that. I made things worse than they had to be. I apologize for that."

"Is that why you wanted me to come here? Did you want to apologize in front of a witness?" Diane asked.

"I want you to hear and believe that I see things differently than before." Jaime closed both eyes. "You were right when you said that we didn't know how to talk to each other. I'm apologizing because I'm hoping it isn't too late for us. But even if it is, even if you are too hurt to be able to trust me, I want you to understand I am sorry for hurting you. You said you needed to feel assured I wouldn't do the same kinds of things that I did before. I'm trying to tell you that I understand what you are saying."

"I hear that you're sorry." Diane drew a deep breath and turned toward him, "I'm sorry too. I played my part in it as well. I hear that you want me to trust you. I can't go through what happened again. I don't want to do that to myself."

"I don't want that for you either," Jaime said.

Diane slumped into the corner of her chair. She closed her eyes and then turned her head away from Jaime and peered out the window that faced the garden outside.

"I've learned a lot of things over the past months. I want to see if we can get back what we had," Jaime said.

Diane watched Jaime, but she remained silent, listening.

He continued. "You said that you played your part in what happened as well. I really don't understand what your part was. I want to understand what it was like for you." Jaime chewed his lip. He returned Diane's gaze for a moment and then looked back at me.

I said, "Diane, how does it make you feel hearing what Jaime has said about the part he played in what happened?"

"I feel good about what he's saying. At the same time, I don't know if I can trust it. And I can say I had a part in everything that happened, but I don't understand what it was."

"Is it important to you to understand it? Do you want to understand it?" I asked.

"Yes."

"Do you want to work on that here?" I asked.

"If I can. Sure, I want to do that. Jaime's anger still makes me uneasy. In order to work on myself, I need to know I'm not going to have to contend with the threat of being cut off by him again. I may provoke his anger, but he's got to manage it. I need to believe he can do that. That's what I would need to feel safe.

"Even though he walked away from me, it felt like an assault. My confidence in what he felt about me was shattered. I doubted myself, my judgment. I need to understand where that intensity comes from," she said.

Back to the Bridge

"We can explore and try to resolve this further," I said. "I want to review what I said a few sessions ago about how critical the beginning of a conversation is. If we can start well, the chances for it to continue productively improve tremendously. So we need to keep in mind what we want to accomplish. We are going back to the beginning of that talk so we can sift through what happened. And by what happened I don't mean the literal script involving who said what—the first dimension recall of the conversation. We get a chance to examine what was going on under the surface. And in doing that, our purpose is to create emotional safety."

Talk alone—the first dimension, words and their literal meaning, conversation that stays on the surface of our experience—does not have the depth to bring healing. But when we connect on deeper dimensions, we can move between the past and present and address feelings and thoughts that effectively have been put on hold. If we take advantage of the chance, we have the opportunity to complete moments that have been left jagged and unresolved, that cut into and shred our sense of intactness whenever they come to mind. Because they are upsetting, our inclination is to keep them away from awareness, to avoid examining them, because that involves reexperiencing them. These unresolved memories hover within, like in a state of emotional suspended animation, threatening to burst from stop action into play mode upon being recalled. And when they are activated, they can feel scary. But avoidance will not resolve them. The challenge is to approach them without allowing them to flare up into the way they felt originally, which was overwhelming.

Talking things over in an atmosphere of emotional safety can allow us to contemplate what we have experienced, while opening possibilities for reenvisioning what happened in this way: We can think of painful moments in light of how *we might have* experienced them had we had the benefit of information and understandings we have gained since the time of the initial experience. On that basis, we can imagine a different outcome to the original situation. That new outcome can include the completion of behavior that was thwarted in the original experience. Where we had felt vulnerable and defenseless, we can imagine a way in which we might have protected ourselves, for example. Or it might involve reexperiencing a situation in memory in such a way as to decrease its intensity; for example, we can recall a situation that at the time triggered feelings that we might not survive. In reimagining it, we can bridge over to knowing that we did survive. Going through such a process can actually restructure the memory itself and bring great relief. This works clinically in many situations. Numerous trauma theories and techniques take advantage of these principles. It allows us to modify the memory of the painful event so that we are no longer haunted by the terror with which we first experienced it. This is one aspect of the hard work involved in relational healing. We resolve to face the pain with a mind toward healing and moving forward. If we are able to do this and maintain a compassionate attitude, we can succeed in restoring and rebuilding our relationships in direct proportion to our own and our partners' desire to do so. This is one of the ways in which the stage for deep healing gets set.

I spoke softly. "In moments when we are disconnected from others, we often are also disconnected from ourselves. In doing this work, we not only make our relationships more whole and more integrated but also we put our own selves back together when we have a healing dialogue with our partners. Does that make sense to you?"

"That makes sense," Jaime said.

Diane nodded.

I continued. "The processing of emotion, something simple and basic and so mundane that it comes into play every time a decision needs to be made, involves many complex considerations. When we revisit our experiences, like we are doing here, we give ourselves a chance to regather all that went into making the choices we made. And the hope is that *we learn about each other's way of making choices* and about many of the factors that went into making the choices, including those that were invisible at the moment of the actual experience. This is one way we get to know each other on deeper levels. This richness of self-knowledge and knowledge of our partners goes into creating a sense of intimacy, a sense of the uniqueness of the connection shared. We move toward being known and knowing our partners intimately and intricately.

"The value of talking about the past is the payoff in the present. When we know more about our own and our partners' inner experiences, we may understand events we've lived through as meaning something other than what we originally presumed.

"When we engage in this kind of dialogue, three-dimensional conversation, new levels and layers of awareness come into play. Reprocessing the experiences and the memories of those experiences in conversation creates possibilities for us to reprocess them internally. Perspectives that were unrecognized, misrecognized, unresolved, or simply overlooked can be brought into focus and explored productively. For example, Jaime, the conversation about how you would respond to the job offer had a practical component, of course. But as we have discussed, underneath the talk about the job was the issue of trust. Jaime, you have acknowledged that you were not trusting that

Diane had your best interests at heart in that talk. You were experiencing her as trying to control or minimize you.

"Lots of couples who have painful experiences together try to work things out afterward. Sometimes in trying to work it out, what emerges is that the person who is labeled as having committed some act of emotional violence—for the sake of this conversation, consider Jaime's having walked away—comes back and apologizes. The person who walks away may say they want to do things differently, but, other than making the statement, they may offer little or no evidence that they will be different. Unless the apology and implicit request for forgiveness feels genuine, the person who has been hurt will remain unmotivated to move forward in rebuilding trust. If the hurt party accepts the apology while feeling it is inadequate, the couple will not be able to experience a new beginning. If they playact together that things are better when the forgiveness has not been earned, rather than a new beginning they will commit themselves to a false start. For an apology to be effective, the forgiveness must feel 'earned.' Diane, do you have any doubts about Jaime's sincerity?"

"No, I have no doubts about his sincerity. It's about consistency. At least for me it is. I believe in his sincerity. I feel like we are going through something that is healing for us."

"That sounds good," I said. "Jaime, how do you feel?"

"I feel good about what we are doing. I'm more hopeful now than I have been since we started working together."

"Diane watched you walk away and experienced feeling both attacked and defenseless. You, on the other hand, felt she had sided against you, and you wanted to protect your own self. But aside from who was attacking or defending, she asks, 'Where did that intensity come from?' If you were blindsided by your anger and you now regret having unleashed it, what is to prevent you from being blindsided again? If she could understand that reservoir of anger and its connection to her, or its connection to whatever else is relevant, that might help her to recover a feeling that you can be trusted. Even being aware that you may have a repository of anger within, she may feel safe if she understands that you have it under control. In order to control it, Jaime, you'd have to understand it yourself. Right now, it seems the intensity is a mystery, and as long as it stays that way, the chances are that Diane will feel distant. Do I have that right, Diane?"

"Yes, that is how I feel. How can I believe in Jaime not doing it again unless I see that he understands where it came from and that he has a handle on whatever the issues are for him?"

"Jaime does that make sense to you?"

"Yes it makes sense. The thing I remember most clearly, what set me off that night is I felt Diane was telling me that she didn't trust my judgment, or even that she had no respect for it."

"You thought Diane was talking down to you? We've talked about that before," I said.

"That's right," Jaime said. "I thought she was trying to tell me that if she were in my position, she would handle the situation better than I was doing."

"You felt she was doing something that she shouldn't be doing, putting you down and telling you something that she shouldn't be telling you?" I said.

"Exactly," Jaime said.

"And you would have wanted her to say and do things differently. You were angry that she wasn't doing things differently. Right?"

Jaime nodded. "That's right."

"And you wanted her to do better than that, better than what she was doing. Is that right?" I asked.

"It sounds a little funny when you say it that way, but yes."

"You wanted different words and a different perspective than the one she was offering?"

"Yes."

"Do you see where I'm going with this?" I asked.

"I'm not sure," Jaime said.

"You were asking her to tell you something other than what was on her mind. Isn't that very close to what you were saying that she had been doing to you when she responded to your declaration of love for her by asking why you hadn't stated that you wanted her to be the mother of your children? There she said that you had not said the right words or expressed the right perspective, the one that she felt she needed to hear at the moment.

"I'm not wagging my index finger at you and going *Tsk, tsk*, like you broke a rule. What I'm pointing out is that this way of talking—where you feel like you've got to read each other's mind, where one of you is responsible for intuitively knowing exactly what the right or the wrong thing to say will be in a given situation—goes on between you and Diane. This expectation goes back and forth between you. Sometimes she may do it to you, and sometimes you may do it to her."

"I can see that," Jaime said.

"I can see that too," Diane said.

I continued, "So on that night, the conversation had very little evidence of a third dimension, and it drifted toward disconnection, though that still doesn't necessarily account for the intensity of your response, Jaime."

Jaime said nothing.

"One thing that occurs to me is that the core issue was not what she told you, or even her urgency about whether another good job offer would come along," I said. "The deeper issue was whether you trusted that she had your best interest at heart. Because, in effect, *if you give her the benefit of the doubt,* no matter what she said, she was offering you her best thoughts on the issue at hand. If you agreed with her, you could adopt her point of view or allow yourself to be influenced by it. If you disagreed, you could disregard what she said entirely but still give her credit for trying to be helpful. Somehow though, when she offered her opinion, you began to see her as an adversary. That's the part I'd like us to look at."

Jaime said, "Okay, I think I see what you mean. She was giving me what was on her mind, and it wasn't what I was thinking I wanted to hear from her. So I felt it was unhelpful. I felt she should have come up with something that coincided with my point of view, or at least a point of view that would be directly supportive of the way I saw things."

"And for her to be directly supportive of the way you saw things, she would need direct access to the way you saw things—she'd have to be inside your head and be able to read your mind."

Jaime smiled, I believe in recognition of this point. He had complained in other conversations that Diane would be satisfied with him only if he were able to read her mind.

"Instead of seeing things the way you saw them, she saw things her own way. She used her own words and had her own concept of what would further the discussion. When she voiced her thoughts and feelings, you felt not only disappointed but enraged that she had failed to recognize what would have been accepted and appreciated by you as a helpful response," I said.

Jaime leaned forward. "Yes. I can see that. I can see that I was asking her, in a sense, to read my mind. I didn't want her to challenge the way I was thinking about the situation."

"What occurs to me," I said, "is that Diane had a sense that you wouldn't agree with what she had in mind. She knew that her perspective on what you needed to do was not aligned with your thoughts. Nonetheless, she went ahead and confronted you. Perhaps it was a courageous thing for her to do. One way of looking at what happened is that she offered her opinion to you in order to control you or demonstrate a lack of support. You've said you took it that way at first. But perhaps she was willing to risk getting you angry at her because she felt the issue was important and wanted you at least to know where she stood on it, so you could consider your options carefully with the benefit of that information. Is it possible that she weighed in on the issue in order to support you in making the best decision you could? Or did she do it to impede you, to control you because she did not trust that your judgment was adequate to handle what was going on? What do you think about those questions now?"

"Well, I certainly wasn't thinking that what she said on that night was for my benefit. Now when I think about it, I can believe that she wanted to do the best she could for me. I can see that I was not listening in a sympathetic way. I was not thinking about having an emotionally safe conversation. Maybe I had a chip on my shoulder. I felt defensive and got angry. For whatever reason, I was unwilling to give Diane credit for doing the best she could in the moment. I can see that."

"You say, 'for whatever reason'; the crux of what we are talking about right now revolves around what those reasons might be," I said.

Before Jaime could respond, I asked Diane, "How does it feel to hear Jaime describe his response to you this way?"

"It feels different. It feels like if he were thinking along these lines, it might have kept him from getting so angry. If he were able to consider the possibility that I might have been trying in my own way to be supportive—even if he felt I was not very successful in my effort—it might have felt completely different for both of us. I can see that."

Slowing Down the Dialogue

I said, "Can you see that thinking along these lines would be an example of what I keep talking about when I say that you both need to slow down the dialogue? By slowing down, I mean question some of the assumptions you make as you are talking with each other. Basic assumptions, like: Is it reasonable for me to assume that Diane is trying to control me, or that she is casting a vote of no-confidence in me on this issue? Or is it possible that she is simply doing the best she can to articulate her thoughts and feelings with the hope that what she says and does will be useful to me? If you can slow yourself down enough to entertain these perspectives, if you can remind yourself that almost all interpersonal situations have multiple perspectives, it can delay the process of revving up anger. Once you get angry there's no more thinking about whether the way you are thinking is the only way or the best way of handling what is going on. So resisting the triggers gives you more freedom. It never eliminates the possibility that you may become angry in the end, but it gives you more time to work with yourself. You get to consider exactly what we are striving to be able to consider: what the next best move, in terms of creating emotional safety, might be."

"I hear you. But that is hard to do in the moment," Diane said.

Jaime chimed in. "Very hard."

"It's hard, but what happened on that night and the knee-jerk assumptions in the communication process are harder to live with," I said. "If you're looking for a way of communicating that will protect your relationship, this is an option: conversation with mindfulness versus conversation without it. Which is harder? In the long run, life without mindfulness is not only harder but much lonelier. The real question is not which is harder, it's whether mindfulness, three-dimensional communication, is possible. I believe it is, and what's more, I believe you are moving toward it. This is what it feels like. You are moving toward it, working with your feelings rather than avoiding them. Would you agree to that?"

"I would," Diane said.

Jaime nodded, clearly in agreement.

I asked Jaime to think out loud about what he remembered of that night on the bridge.

"Right or not, I felt, that you [Diane] were putting me in a double bind. Because you are the one I go to for support in being the person I want to be. I look to you to bolster me when I want to take chances and reach for my dreams. And it felt like you'd stopped believing in me. You wanted me to take a job I didn't want. So I was angry."

"So you felt like you were looking for encouragement to take chances and that Diane was telling you to play it safe," I said.

"Something like that. I was looking to go out there and test myself, find out who I was. And Diane wasn't supporting me. That reminded me of conversations I'd had with my dad. He was good to me, but what he wanted for me and what I wanted for myself were two different things. To him, the most important thing was a *steady* paycheck, with the emphasis on steady, not paycheck. That's what his work experience had been. And if that was good enough for him, he wanted me to feel that it was good enough for me, or at least this is the way I understood it. If I liked what I was doing or felt like I was engaged in learning something, that didn't mean anything to him. For him a job was a shield against desperation. For whatever reason, aiming for something else didn't compute, or it didn't compute when he thought of me.

"He's a good man. But I wanted something else. I always wanted something different, and I felt like I went after it. He didn't want me go into advertising, but then he didn't want me to leave it. He didn't want me to go back to school. Excitement or adventure or creativity as part of the work experience was foreign to him, to the point that he felt it was even a little suspicious or pretentious or something. Like it wasn't what I was brought up to think. As a matter of fact, during a conversation we had about job satisfaction, he rolled his eyes. In any case, I thought I had what I needed in my work in advertising. But at some point, I started feeling like I had the same kind of job my father had. Aside from the money, there was nothing in it for me. I wanted something else. So it was like I'm in this struggle with him my whole life. And then I'm hearing you [Diane] say what you did, I felt like you were siding with him and telling me to take the sure thing. Anything more and you're putting on airs, or you are just plain foolish."

Diane clasped her hands. "I didn't mean it that way. But I can understand how you would take it that way. I can see how you might think that I was telling you not to reach higher." She paused, seeming to gather her thoughts. "I wasn't thinking of that job as a dead end. I see that you saw it that way, but I wasn't thinking that. I had confidence that if you took it, it would not keep you pinned down. I have great confidence in you to keep moving and growing."

As if he hadn't heard her, Jaime said, "It's funny, but to me, it would be like if I told you that you needed to stop thinking about dance or having kids, and said, 'Just feel good about what you are doing now.' Or if I'd said that you should go back to school for something that you didn't have any passion to do. And I feel committed not to doing that. As long as your dream centers on dance, I support you in doing whatever you can to move in that direction. You're the one who has to be in charge of changing what your goals are."

"I appreciate that," Diane said.

"Those are your dreams, not just of what you want to do but of who you are," Jaime said. "You're entitled to pursue them. I want our relationship to be a refuge from doubt or negativity about whether either of us can reach for our dreams." He paused before continuing. "So you can see how confusing it was for me to think that you were telling me, 'Forget about whatever vague stuff you are thinking. Go with the sure thing.'"

"Yes, I can see that," Diane said.

"That's how and why I felt betrayed by you," Jaime said. "I want you to believe in me and let me know that. I want you to trust me and also believe that I will have your back and take care of practical matters. Because I have come through in the practical stuff."

Diane stared at him. I couldn't read her feelings and thoughts right then and wasn't sure if Jaime had finished speaking.

Then he continued. "I know that I make mistakes. I know, for example, that I was out of control with my drinking, and I was helpless to control it by myself. But I turned that around before we got together. I got help when I needed it. I want that to mean something to you. I want you to believe in me and know that you can rely on me. I will do what I need to do for myself, and for you, and for us. I want to feel your confidence in me. And the reason I want to feel it is because I want to be with you. I want it to be me and you together."

"When you make that point," I said, "it's as if you were angry because Diane, from your point of view, had caused you to stop believing that she wanted to stay within the core of your relationship with you. You felt betrayed because in your mind she was not affirming confidence in your ability to go out and do something more challenging and different from accepting the job offer. Is that accurate?"

"Yes, that's what I'm saying," Jaime said.

I turned to Diane. "How does it make you feel to hear this? What he wants from you?"

"It makes me feel bad and good." She faced Jaime. "I do want to be there for you, Jaime. I don't want to be like your father. I really don't. I get frightened sometimes, though. Maybe because I feel like my creative work is so far behind where I'd like it to be. When I heard about your job offer, I felt like we, *you and me*, could have some security and that it might be our ticket to having a family together. I want to stop worrying about what the next steps are going to be for us. Listening to you speak about what it felt like to you makes me feel like maybe that was selfish of me. I don't know. Maybe—just like you talk about being patient with me and not pushing me to close out on my dreams of finding a place in the dance world unless I make my own decision about that. It's not my place to tell you to close out your dreams— whether I understand them or even whether you understand them completely. I didn't mean to make you feel that I was giving up on you. In my heart I didn't feel I was doing that."

"Jamie, how does it feel to hear Diane say what she just said about her relationship with you?"

"I feel like we've come a long way together to get to this place. I feel like we believe in each other more than we were able to understand before. We didn't know how to understand how connected we really are.

"Thinking about it now, Diane, I don't understand what you could have or should have done differently. I don't think you did anything wrong. At the time I thought you were cornering me, but maybe I was the one cornering you by leaving you and walking away. What I did, walking away, was self-protective, but it cost me plenty. It hurt you badly, which of course ended up hurting me."

"Because you were the one leaving and Diane had no option for connecting, is that how you mean that she was cornered?" I asked.

"That's right," Jaime said. "I blamed you [Diane] and was angry at you for not understanding me. Instead I could have tried to help you understand me better. That's what I want our relationship and our communication process to be about."

"I want that too." Diane reached over and took Jaime's hand.

"That's how I want to feel about us," Jaime said. "I don't know for sure if we can do it because I've never really had that with anyone. It's new territory. But when I think about the good things we have experienced together, I say to myself, 'Our good times are my best times.' Why can't we help each other through any- and everything? If you want to do that, then I know we have a chance."

Diane's cheeks glistened with tears.

Jaime told Diane that more than anything else he hoped he could stop hurting her with his anger. And stop hurting himself by letting it out without thinking about what the effects would be.

"Controlling anger and limiting its destructive effects is necessary, and damage control is important," I said. "But in and of itself, reducing anger does not create emotional safety. It makes it more likely and possible for emotional safety to emerge. Cultivating heightened awareness of the triggers that cause anger is key to managing it. Anger management is important for many partners and crucial for some. Three-dimensional communication and emotional safety is necessary for all."

EXERCISE 7.1

Deep Communication

How do you go about creating the conditions that will allow your partner to feel he is being heard? That is what this exercise is designed to help you do. First, I'll define two aspects of the most common conflict situations I encounter in my work. Most couples think that these aspects are the most important features of their dialogue and want to work them out in detail. I am going to help you define these aspects and then ask you to set them aside as we consider other features of the dialogue that, in fact, merely camouflage the aspects that offer us the greatest chance to build emotional safety. What I hope to do in this exercise is help you uncover what these are. Prepare to tolerate a mild amount of confusion as you figure out where we are headed. The path will become very clear in a short period of time. And when it does, the result will be worth the effort.

First, think of a situation in which you and your partner do not see eye to eye. Describe the disagreement in neutral terms. Do not explain or justify your point of view here, simply describe the issues at hand.

_____

_____

I will refer to your description of the disagreement as Part A.

Now jot down the reason(s) you feel your perspective is correct and your partner's is flawed.

_____

_____

I'll refer to your understanding of the essence of why you feel your perspective is correct and your partner's is flawed as Part B.

The key point for this exercise is that neither Part A nor Part B is crucial to what is necessary for overcoming this disagreement and integrating it into a three-dimensional dialogue!

How you listen and respond to each other is critical.

Leave Part A and Part B on the side as you work through this exercise.

Consider Parts A and B as distractions from the task at hand, which is to create emotional safety. If for any reason at this point you feel like you would be unable to do that, express the reasons why this would be difficult for you below:

_____

_____

_____

If you have written anything I will refer to that statement as Part C.

Many partners have reasons they cannot proceed in learning how to conduct a nonjudgmental dialogue with their partners. For the purposes of this exercise, it is necessary that you release yourself from the obligation of identifying with Parts B and C. After the exercise is over, of course, you can reclaim them. To benefit, please put them aside for the moment if you can.

Summary:

Part A = description of the disagreement

Part B = the reason(s) you feel you are correct and your partner's perspective is flawed

Part C = the reason(s), if you have any, why you feel it would be impossible to talk about the disagreement without bringing up the fact that your perspective is right and your partner's is wrong

So now imagine that you invite your partner to describe how he feels about this issue. It is important that he understands that you are not asking him to engage in a debate with you. You are not trying to set the stage for him to persuade or convince you to agree with him.

The Three-Dimensional Communication Stance

Explain that you want right now to immerse yourself in understanding how he feels about the situation from his perspective, and that you are not asking about his perspective in order to evaluate or criticize it. This is the deep listening, three-dimensional communication stance.

Consider carefully what this means for you as a listener. It means that if you feel an urge to correct your partner, you are committed to resisting that urge. Should you feel the urge to debate any specific point, please don't. The purpose of your listening is so that your partner can experience his thoughts and emotions within himself and also feel that those thoughts and feelings are being transmitted by him and received by you.

It's important that you are clear that you don't have to agree with what your partner is saying. What you are doing is helping him share his perspective. By partaking of it, you validate his thoughts and feelings as real with no commitment intended or implied as far as agreeing with him.

The time to focus on your reaction to the content of what he is saying has a place in the communication process, but this is not it.

Imagine how you might feel *if you understood his experience as he does.* That is what you are reaching toward: to come as close as you can to understanding his experience as he does.

You can allow his inside view to come into your own inner perspective!

And if you can allow that to happen and verbally/nonverbally convey that you are listening in this uncritical, noncompetitive, and accepting way, this brings emotional safety to the fore.

Supplementary Concerns and
Common Questions

What does deep listening offer your partner? Compassionate attention. Human understanding. Interpersonal resonance. Empathy. Respect. All of these things are more important than either Parts B or C.

A disagreement handled skillfully can become a benchmark for demonstrating your commitment to emotional safety and loving compassion.

You and your partner can learn to listen to each other in this way. Feeling heard means feeling you are not alone. Feeling not alone makes problem solving easier. Knots loosen. Life becomes full of solutions to problems that formerly had been considered insoluble.

This exercise is designed to help you think about what deep communication entails and to avoid going at loggerheads with your partner when you disagree.

What if your partner isn't interested in learning this method? The method works best if both partners engage in it. If for any reason only one partner is agreeable to participating, the exercise can still provide a powerful benefit.

Do you have a vampire argument in your relationship? Can you think of an argument with your partner that has no real life in it but never seems to die? An argument does not come to any resolution but simply repeats a pattern that feels deadening. This method will help you to break the deadlock and open up the issue to a productive resolution. At the heart of these "dead" conversations lies a chronic feeling, usually both partners share it, that neither partner is being heard.

How do you look when you listen? When you listen to your partner, you need to demonstrate by your expression and your posture that you are interested in what he is saying.

EXERCISE 7.2

Four Relational Quadrants

This exercise will enable you to chart resilience and closeness in your relationship. It is an excellent tool for providing a quick view of the direction your relationship appears to be moving.

Where is your relationship now? And where is it heading?

Graph the Direction of Your Relationship

Using the Axis of Affection/Closeness and Conversational Resilience

The theory of three-dimensional communication encourages partners to think about their relationship from multiple perspectives. In any given situation, we have a tool for analyzing communication between partners. This three-dimensional analysis answers the questions: How clear are partners' messages? How well do they convey the meaning each partner intends? How aware are the partners of each other's rhythm—by that I mean the speed with which they receive and integrate new messages in the relationship? What are the feelings underneath the words? And what does the interaction in the here and now indicate regarding opportunities to create emotional safety or to reverse a damaging trend?

Let's compare this with and contrast it to other perspectives that can be helpful. Let's consider the *primary view* to be the perspective we use when making face-to-face contact. Partners communicate about here and now issues in terms of what they perceive, think, and feel in the moment and about the moment.

The *secondary view* is when partners compare and contrast the here and now with the trends within the relationship to evaluate direction. Is the communication moving them toward or away from the goals they hope to reach together? That secondary view might be considered an overhead view. It is derived not from looking into your partner's eye but from consulting your own mind's eye; the secondary view takes a past-present-future view of the relationship as process.

Many couples automatically focus on one of these two perspectives, but it is important to integrate them. Considering relationship in the third dimension implies an integration of these perspectives.

People think about relationships in many different ways. Some hear words as they think, some see pictures, and some have little sensitivity to how their thought process flows. The styles people develop, in terms of their thinking and feeling, are complex and fascinating. In deference to the enormous variation in intellectual and emotional processing, I am sure that the following schema will feel natural to some and counterintuitive to others.

Some couples find the schema baffling. Others take to it immediately and have informed me that it helped them achieve a breakthrough in understanding the three-dimensional perspective. With that in mind, I offer it to you:

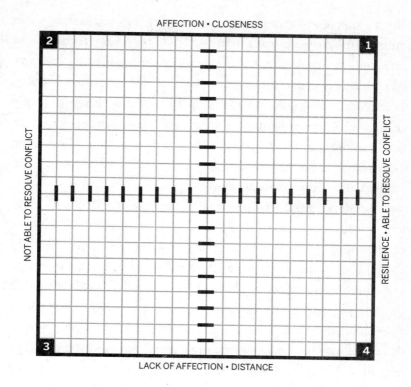

AFFECTION · CLOSENESS

NOT ABLE TO RESOLVE CONFLICT

RESILIENCE · ABLE TO RESOLVE CONFLICT

LACK OF AFFECTION · DISTANCE

QUADRANT ONE

This couple feels good about one another and, should they argue, can resolve differences effectively.

QUADRANT TWO

This couple feels close and affectionate but becomes alienated from one another whenever conflict arises. They are unable to resolve differences without degrading trust and mutual comfort level.

QUADRANT THREE

This couple neither feels close nor affectionate nor do they have the ability to resolve conflicts without hurting each other's feelings.

QUADRANT FOUR

This couple's feelings of closeness and affection, if they ever existed, have cooled off. When differences arise, however, they can mediate them effectively without becoming hostile to one another.

This simple graph has two axes: one going vertical and the other horizontal. The two variables that correspond to the distance from the null spot (the neutral spot at the center of the graph) are as follows: the vertical distance is a measure of the level of affection and closeness a couple feels about their relationship. This variable is measured on a scale that runs from positive to negative ten. If a couple is positioned with a ten for the first variable, they have self-rated their affection and closeness levels as being very high; a minus ten on the other hand would indicate that the couple has great animosity toward each other.

The second variable corresponds to the ease or lack of ease that a couple has in repairing a disagreement or disappointment between them. Think of it as resilience. This variable also can be positive or negative and runs from one to ten either above or below the neutral (zero) point. For those who easily see each other's viewpoint and are able to convey empathic understanding without relinquishing their authentic perspectives, the rating is likely to be a positive ten. For those who find that even the most trivial disagreements escalate into trust-damaging arguments, the rating on this variable would be negative, at or close to negative ten.

In the First Quadrant we find couples who feel good about each other and are able to resolve differences effectively when problems arise. I do not see many of these couples in my private practice or in my work as clinical supervisor and codirector of the Family and Couples Treatment Service (FACTS), a division of the Institute for Contemporary Psychotherapy in Manhattan.

In the Second Quadrant are partners who are able to enjoy their lives together but can easily fall prey to minor disagreements exploding into major upsets. These couples often come in for couples therapy. When couples like this wait too long before coming in for couples work, the feeling of disappointment and despair about solving the central communication problems often becomes so ingrained that satisfaction with the relationship itself dwindles considerably by the time they actually come in to work on improving their communication. Eventually, difficulties sap the positive feeling completely, and couples in the Second Quadrant would then slide down into the Third Quadrant.

In the Third Quadrant we find partners who no longer, if they ever did, feel good about each other or their relationship. They also have little ability to repair issues, talk things through, or come to productive understandings. These couples have a hard time tracking where they are. Once you slip into this quadrant, it's easy to lose track of how far you are from being able to regain positive feelings about the relationship. It is easy for a couple, for example, who ranks a negative two in the first variable to *feel* like they are a negative eight or even a nine or ten. That's because once you dip into the negative numbers, you rarely, if ever, get the support or boost that comes from a successful interaction with your partner. You have so infrequently seen eye to eye with your partner that you begin to doubt whether such a thing is possible anymore. Perhaps this is the type of client I have worked with more than any other throughout my career. So my work with couples in this quadrant often begins with a focus on helping them to understand what the possibility of reviving hopefulness might mean for them. For some, this phase of the work is uplifting, as they get to see that they are not as far from possibilities for feeling better together as they might have imagined. For others, the degree of trust that has withered or completely decomposed is depressing; the order of business, in terms of relational healing, becomes grieving for possibilities and opportunities for positive change that have already been squandered.

Quadrant Four couples sometimes come for treatment. Often these partners have already come to a decision that they are not suited to one another, but they want to figure out what happened. If they can speak with each other frankly, their communication process has strong points. They have made some conscious decisions that have involved or caused significant distance between them. They may not have regrets about the state of their relationship, but, in spite of that, there is often confusion. If the partners are going to separate, they want to do so on good terms. With couples in this situation, sometimes discussion of the reasons they began to feel bad about the relationship produces resolution of those feelings and results in such an improvement that they are able to rise into the First Quadrant. This does not always happen, but it presents itself as a real possibility with some Quadrant Four couples—again depending on how negative that first variable is.

Following are illustrations of how to use the graph.

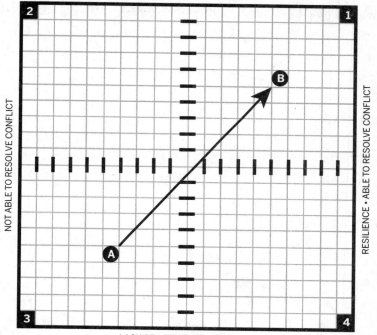

CHET & MILO

AFFECTION · CLOSENESS

NOT ABLE TO RESOLVE CONFLICT

RESILIENCE · ABLE TO RESOLVE CONFLICT

LACK OF AFFECTION · DISTANCE

A After three years together   **B** After five years together

(-4, -5) Chet & Milo after three years together . . .

Chet was thirty-two and Milo two years his senior at the time I first met this couple. They were furious with each other and highly distrustful. Any conflict seemed to expand into a large impasse. The low rating in closeness and affection appeared to have much to do with their inability to stabilize whether they wanted a committed monogamous or an open relationship. Neither had been in a relationship, previous to this one, that had lasted more than six months. Each felt that there was a lot at stake and did want to work on making their relationship better.

(5, 5) Chet & Milo after five years together . . .

This couple was able to turn around the downward trend in their relationship. Both entered into individual therapy and they sought out couples therapy as well. For them, having an open relationship was something they, in theory, may have felt good about trying but, in practice, felt uncomfortable with. Their worst fights and deepest wounds seemed to all emanate from issues related to a "third" person. And once the equilibrium of the relationship was disturbed, which was early on, deciding on the style of a new piece for the living room ended in accusations and name calling.

LORRAINE & STEVE

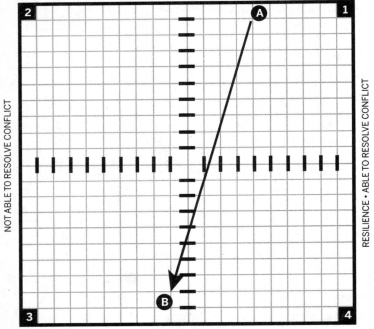

AFFECTION • CLOSENESS

NOT ABLE TO RESOLVE CONFLICT

RESILIENCE • ABLE TO RESOLVE CONFLICT

LACK OF AFFECTION • DISTANCE

A Six months after marriage   **B** Four years later

(9, 4) Lorraine & Steve six months after marriage . . .

As newlyweds Lorraine and Steve, both thirty years of age, were wildly enamored of one another. Their time together began like an extended party. That explains the first parameter of 9 for feelings of affection and closeness. The positive rating for resilience, for them, indicated that they were able to work around any problems. At this phase, however, stress was minimal and an underlying inability to negotiate differences had yet to surface.

(2, -1) Lorraine & Steve four years later . . .

Steve's company downsized and he found himself out of a job. Instead of sympathizing with and encouraging him, he felt that Lorraine questioned his professional competence. What's more, although he harbored resentments, he kept them to himself. They grew emotionally distant from one another. She suspected he was having an affair. His bouts of heavy drinking further eroded trust. The affection and closeness index plummeted dramatically. Lorraine felt unsafe and unloved. Steve appeared to feel numb and chronically angry. Interestingly, in spite of these challenging conditions, this couple responded well to couples therapy.

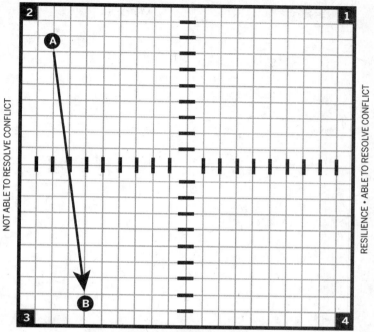

JOY & TONY

AFFECTION · CLOSENESS

NOT ABLE TO RESOLVE CONFLICT

RESILIENCE · ABLE TO RESOLVE CONFLICT

LACK OF AFFECTION · DISTANCE

A After one year   **B** One year later

(7, -8) Joy & Tony after living together for one year . . .

Joy in her midthirties and Tony in his early forties enjoyed a brief honeymoon period but when the infatuation started to wear off they had little developed in their dialogue to help them cope with the stresses of adult living. Joy had wished them to begin couples therapy but Tony resisted. He felt that if they cared enough about each other they should be able to work their problems out on their own. Both wanted children, but Tony was adamant about putting that off for quite a while. Joy didn't want to wait.

(-8, -6) Joy & Tony after living together for two years . . .

This couple broke up after two years of living together and left one another on poor terms.

CARA & KEITH

AFFECTION · CLOSENESS

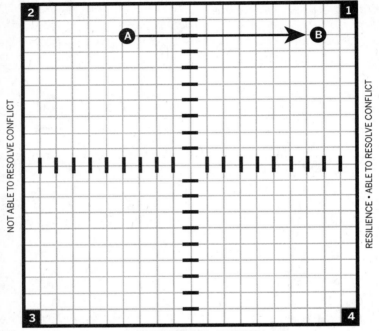

LACK OF AFFECTION · DISTANCE

A After one year together **B** After three years

(8, -4) Cara & Keith after one year of living together . . .

Cara and Keith, in their midthirties, enjoy one another's company, report great sex, and each is excited about the other's talents and personality. However, both feel misunderstood and that the other lacks the patience or emotional sensitivity to help them to be known, feel known.

(8, 7) Cara & Keith after three years of living together . . .

This couple was able to show success with a combination of good changes and good fortune. Each began to take off in their separate careers, each got involved in meditation and yoga practices and were able to spend time together feeling safe and successful. Although they had fought constantly a few years ago, each had a way of controlling the level of conflict so that neither felt devastated, only disconnected when things were bad. A year of couples therapy helped them to develop a language and method for working out disagreements more productively.

Use the quadrants to chart the direction of your relationship in the following exercise. How would you rate your current relationship in terms of the two variables?

Write down your estimate of the degree of *Affection and Closeness* you are currently experiencing with your partner: _____

_____

_____

_____.

And note your estimate of this variable as of four months ago:

_____

_____.

Write down your estimate of the degree of *Resilience* you are currently experiencing with your partner: _____

_____

_____.

And note your estimate of this variable as of four months ago:

_____

_____.

Current Affection: _____

_____.

Current Resilience: _____

_____.

Affection four months ago: _____

_____.

Resilience four months ago: _____

_____.

Plot these points on the graph below:

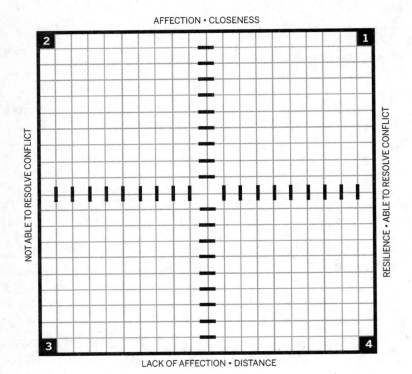

What quadrant are you currently in? _____
_____.

Where were you four months ago? _____
_____.

How do you account for the change if there is one? _____
_____.

If no change, how do you understand that? _____
_____.

CHAPTER EIGHT

Twenty Questions

Trust is the glue of life. It's the most essential ingredient in effective communication. It's the foundational principle that holds all relationships.

—Stephen Covey

What do clients take away with them from couples therapy? What do they find most useful? What inspires realistic hope?

Research validates that psychotherapy is helpful to clients, but there is no consensus on the precise elements that make it so. The answers to the questions above are controversial.

Certain moments, certain interchanges between therapist and client(s) provide what is needed to make breakthroughs possible. These moments can seem incidental in that their occurrence is neither predictable nor guaranteed. Yet they occur, and sometimes frequently. In the three-dimensional communication approach to couples therapy, the ability to envision, conceptualize, formulate, and strategize to bring about emotional safety is highlighted. How and when in the process do these breakthroughs come about, take hold, and grow?

In this chapter I provide twenty statements posed in various ways. Each originated with a client's comment or question. I invite you to read and respond to the items. This chapter is designed to provide you with a springboard to help you express your views and feelings about the various elements of the communication process. The items and your responses comprise Section One of the exercise. In Section Two I respond to the same items myself. I invite you to compare and contrast my responses with your own. My hope is that the chapter will feel like we have shared our responses collaboratively.

I used these items as a jumping-off point because each in its own way provides an opportunity for me to share a guideline or to clarify a notion that may have sparked a breakthrough for the client or her partner at the time.

If you have a partner who would be interested in participating in this exercise, the experience could be helpful and interesting for you both, as long as you maintain an emphasis on creating emotional safety.

Let's suppose that for a series of complex reasons most of us might readily agree to, we all have blind spots in our ability to perceive what is going on between ourselves and others. How do we become aware of them? My hope is that by reviewing some of these basics of communication, this chapter can serve to help you become aware of what your blind spots may be. For this reason, I approach similar questions from a variety of vantage points because, in my experience, blind spots are more likely to center on elemental issues. How do you bring awareness to problems or limitations that you may not have been aware were (or are) a part of your perspective? The method I use here creates an interactive exchange in which you and I can review some of the moving parts in the communication schema together.

If you have questions or comments about the chapter, I encourage you to reach out to me at Babitsm@gmail.com. I will respond to your communication.

The space provided after each item will give you an opportunity to "think out loud" and explore your feelings and thoughts about the statements. If you need more space than I've provided, please have extra paper handy.

Section One

1) There is basically one correct way to interpret any given statement. I usually get exactly what my partner is saying to me.
   Do you agree or disagree? Please elaborate.

2) My partner says something to me, and as a result I feel a certain way. That means that my partner wanted me to feel that way.
   Do you feel this communication stance is reasonable or unreasonable? To what extent do you agree or disagree with it?

3) I listen to the words and forget about the way the words are said. That's the best way to make sure I understand what my partner is trying to get across. That's because he has trouble sounding warm and can easily sound angrier than he feels.
   Does this statement make sense to you? Do you identify with this situation? Please elaborate.

4) I listen to my partner's tone of voice and then judge what she says accordingly. The words are less important than the tone of voice.

    Do you identify with this statement? If you were to change it to represent your view accurately, how would it read?

5) I speak my mind and I expect my partner to do the same. I am not responsible for figuring out what my partner says if he is unable to make it clear.

    Do you identify with this statement? If so, to what extent? Please elaborate your perspective.

6) My partner does as well as she can to get her point across. However, if I don't really understand what she means, it's up to me to ask questions.

    To what extent do you identify with this statement? How would you characterize this person's conversational stance? Describe how it is similar or dissimilar to your own.

7) My partner has a responsibility to find out whether the message he is trying to get across to me is adequate. If I understand what he says in my own way and it's different from what he intended, that's not my fault or responsibility.

Do you identify with the attitude expressed in this statement? Does this represent the way you feel? To what extent do you agree or disagree? Please elaborate.

8) My partner tests me frequently. I believe she asks me to do things to exercise control or evaluate whether I care enough to do what she asks. I believe her motive is to get reassurance, but, nonetheless, I am furious that she plays games like this with me.

   Do you identify with the statement above? Have you ever had a similar experience? How did you feel about it? Were you able to have a productive dialogue with your partner about it?

9) My partner talks nonstop. If uninterrupted, he can go on indefinitely. Aside from not being able to get a word in edgewise, there is no room for me to develop my own perspective through a back-and-forth conversation.

   Do you identify with this situation? What is your feeling about the relative length of time you and your partner talks? Does one or the other dominate conversation? Do you keep track of whether your partner is getting the time he needs to get his point across?

10) Generally speaking, good communication is a matter of intelligence.

What do you think? Please elaborate.

11) Good communication comes from a combination of attention and emotional and cognitive skills.

    Agree or disagree? Please elaborate.

12) Good communication is within the grasp of any person who desires to connect with his partner.

    To what extent do you agree or disagree, and why?

13) Good communication can be foiled by too much fear and anxiety.

    Agree? Disagree? Please elaborate.

14) Good communication can make it easier for a partner to bear her fear or anxiety.

    Does this statement represent the way you feel about good communication? Please elaborate.

15) In a good relationship it is important for both partners to say what is on their minds when they are feeling it.

Please elaborate on the extent to which this statement mirrors your own feelings, or the ways in which it does not.

16) A good communicator is responsible for the way his messages are received.
    What do you think about this statement? Do you identify with it? Please elaborate.

17) People say what they mean to say. If someone makes a statement, she is responsible for the meaning of the words she said.
    Agree? Disagree? Please elaborate.

18) Couples should represent what they feel forcefully in order to be understood. The worst flaw in couples' communication occurs when dialogue is filled with noncommittal statements.
    Agree or not? Please elaborate.

19) Blurting out your feelings is always a mistake.
    Agree or not? Please elaborate.

20) The longer you hold back from talking about something you feel, the more you infect your communication process with resentment.

What do you think about this perspective? Please elaborate.

Section Two

1) There is basically one correct way to interpret any given statement. I usually understand exactly what my partner is saying to me.

Most often, insistence on only one correct vantage point is used in the service of making judgments/accusations. Getting beyond assigning blame for problems in the relationship and focusing on how problems can be addressed collaboratively has much greater potential for healing. There is often more than one correct way to see a situation, given that each of us views it from our unique perspective.

The statement implies that once a partner has arrived at the "correct" perspective, her judgment should be accepted as infallible, with no implied interest in an exchange of perspectives, but only the acceptance of the one perspective she endorses.

Having said this, I want to add a caveat for one-sided situations that can arise. For example, in the event of infidelity, there is a stage in which accountability and clarity about who violated the relational contract can be and often is essential to the possibility of a healing process. Forgiveness in this situation hinges on working through the sense of violation and must be earned. Nonetheless, although anger and blame may be justified in these situations, there is no excuse for cruelty coming from either side. Eventually, a compassionate, non-judgmental acceptance must be reestablished if the relationship is to truly overcome the injuries to attachment.

Who is right and who is wrong, even when infidelity is the issue, can eventually give way to questions concerning matters other than blame and accountability. Repairing damage that has affected both partners is a long process. And although it is not easy, partners do succeed in working through it.

It is not that the perspective of who is right or wrong is unreal or wrong. In terms of couples work, the point is that it is most often a dead end. It does not help to start or maintain a healing process. The better question becomes, "How can the healing be initiated?"

As far as a partner saying that she usually understands exactly what her partner is saying to her, I think on its own it is an admirable accomplishment. Coupled with the first part of the comment, however, it makes me wonder whether it is an empty presumption. If there is only one correct way to see a situation, presumably the person making the statement is asserting that the way in which she understands (or "gets") her partner is the only way her partner can be understood. This can be extended into a statement like "Anyone who disagrees with the way I see things is wrong." It sounds similar to statements like "I'm not telling you my opinion, I'm telling you the way things are. If you dare to disagree, you are either crazy or stupid. And, on top of that, certainly wrong!" Beware of too much certitude. It often masks a chaotic insecurity layered over with defensiveness. Confidence can be a great strength. But too much certainty often signals inflexibility or rigidity; and neither of those qualities promises much in the way of compassion, love, and understanding. They are obstacles to the development of three-dimensional communication.

2) My partner says something to me, and as a result I feel a certain way. That means that my partner wanted me to feel that way.

Separating the impact of what has been said from the intent of the speaker is a very important communication skill. Insistence that the connection between how you feel and what has been said is fixed leaves no room for understanding the entire range of possible miscommunication or misinterpretation that might have occurred and might have led you to possibly misconstrue your partner's intent. It also precludes the possibility of uncovering new information that may change the context or meaning of what was communicated. This is not to say that if you feel bad about something your partner said to you that his motive is always blameless; but the point is that very often the "hurting" part of a remark comes into play through an association or implication that may or may not reflect what the speaker had in mind. In many instances exploring what was meant, rather than presuming to know the other's intention without discussing it, avoids a lot of unnecessary conflict and pain.

This statement embodies a listening stance that exempts the listener from accountability for actively and mindfully exploring the message received.

3) I listen to the words and forget about the way the words are said. That's the best way to make sure I understand what my partner is trying to get across. That's because he has trouble sounding warm and can easily sound angrier than he really is.

This kind of statement is tricky. There are situations in which it may be not only reasonable but insightful and compassionate to take this position. On the other hand, it can cause glitches in communication.

The statement points to a split between the first and second dimensions in the way a partner's messages come across. The partner who is described as sounding angrier than he is may be just that, less angry than he sounds. In that case, the statement is reasonable and appropriate.

There is also a chance that the person who makes allowances for the angry-sounding partner is in denial about the anger in the voice he hears.

Another possibility is that both partners are in denial about the anger that goes back and forth between them and are colluding in mutual avoidance of a problem.

I worked with a couple, Lois and Rachel, whose presenting problem had to do with Lois's discomfort with Rachel's communication style, notably, her loud voice. Lois complained that unless they were alone, their conversations were always public because Rachel could be heard far and wide. Even when they were alone, Lois felt that Rachel's conversation had an impersonal quality because it was not attuned to the fact that Lois appreciated being spoken to in soft tones. Lois interpreted Rachel's loudness as aggressive and angry.

Rachel resented being asked to lower her voice. She claimed that she had always spoken this way, that it was natural to her, and she was not "doing" anything purposefully to upset Lois. She felt that Lois was picking on her and did not believe that the real issue was her voice but something else that was going on with Lois—either having to do with herself or perhaps not. Rachel claimed she had spoken in this manner for as long as she could remember. But, in fact, she did not recall much of her early childhood. As we got to know each other, she recounted the following sequence of events:

When Rachel was three, her parents divorced and she had no contact with her father throughout her childhood and adolescence. Up to that point, her mother was a constant presence in the home. With the divorce, however, came the need for immediate full-time employment. Rachel's mother was out of the house for long stretches of time and came home exhausted. An aunt moved in to try to help out with Rachel and her older sister, Joyce, but the aunt also worked full-time, and the young girls were home alone many hours during the week.

Joyce, five years older than Rachel, was Rachel's main companion, confidante, and contact with family. Joyce had contracted acute rheumatic fever at age seven and suffered severe hearing loss. Although she had no memory of doing so, Rachel reasoned that she had begun speaking loudly at this time to maintain as close contact with her sister as possible. She recalled times while in elementary school when she was home alone. At those times, she conducted solitary dialogues in which she shouted out her part of the conversation and then would improvise responses she imagined her sister might offer if she had been there.

Rachel became aware of her connection between speaking loudly and feeling connected. Once upon a time it had been obvious, but it had become buried under the mass of subsequent experience. Lois saw that as well. Rachel confessed tearfully that she had interpreted Lois's requests that she speak softly as cruel and insensitive attacks. They had made her feel like a child who was being picked on. She had resisted taking them seriously because thinking about them made her feel fragile and needy. Until we spoke about it together, the connection between loud talking and defending against loneliness had never occurred to her. Gradually, the issue shifted in her thinking; she was able to reconfigure Lois's request that she speak in a lower voice as a request to connect with greater intimacy and to fend off loneliness, not as a withering criticism. Speaking softly with Lois, Rachel realized, represented something quite similar to what speaking loudly with Joyce had represented: connection.

Once Lois understood the context in which Rachel's communication pattern had developed, her feeling about the issue changed. Lois apologized for making Rachel feel attacked and criticized.

Although it is hard not to jump to conclusions when we are confronted with situations we find difficult to deal with, we often receive great rewards in terms of improved understanding and intimacy and in cultivating the patience to allow for deeper exploration.

The same statement above would apply in a very different way to Marie and James, partners who both feared open expressions of anger. In the first session I had with them, they informed me that they never fought. Despite having said that, each had a list of grievances that seemed inexhaustible. They were alienated from each other in numerous respects, rarely affectionate or sexually intimate, though before they had moved in together—a year and a half prior to coming in to see me—each reported enjoying and looking forward to their frequent shared sexual experiences.

Marie spoke to James softly, but he replied with gruff, often unelaborated single syllable utterances. In the interest of "keeping the peace," they were in a pattern of avoiding each other. Each feared that open discussion of their anger might bring their relationship to an end. I saw my job as helping them address the notion that if they didn't learn how to speak to each other more openly about what was going on, their chances for survival as a couple would likely dissipate. Although I do emphasize the destructive potential of anger in numerous sections of this book, there are certainly times when expression and resolution of anger cannot be, and should not be, avoided.

For this couple, the willingness to ignore the tone of the message was simply a collusion in the denial of anger issues that neither felt ready or able to deal with.

Evaluating the meaning of a behavior without understanding the context in which it develops often leads partners, or anyone for that matter, to dubious conclusions.

4) I listen to the tone of voice my partner is using and then judge what she says accordingly. The words are less important than the tone of voice.

This statement flips the emphasis of the previous item. Here the tone of voice is claimed to trump the importance of the content, the words that are spoken. Both content and tone are important. And the relationship between the one and the other is crucial. Are content and tone coherent, or do they contradict each other? I often find myself giving the underlying emotion of a statement more weight because it is too often not taken into consideration. Dimension one is content. Without the complement of dimension two, the content is difficult to comprehend. Many partners overemphasize the literal meaning of what is said and ignore the underlying emotional elements. My goal is to rebalance the elements; activating the third dimension demands this. Therefore, I believe that although an overstatement as written here, this item represents an important perspective.

5) I speak my mind and I expect my partner to do the same. I am not responsible for figuring out what my partner says if he is unable to make it clear.

Speaking your mind and expecting your partner to do the same makes sense. Renouncing responsibility for understanding what your partner is saying to you doesn't.

Communication is a collaborative venture. If you do not understand what your partner has tried to get across, why wouldn't you ask him to clarify? You have a responsibility to *yourself*, your partner, and the relationship to do what you can to maintain connection.

Creating emotional safety to the greatest extent possible sometimes demands that you extend yourself. Dialogue sometimes requires questioning and exploring of themes to ensure that both partners develop mutual understanding. Sometimes it can be hard to distinguish between what it means to extend, rather than overextend, yourself.

If the person making the comment above feels that his partner is deliberately sabotaging the communication, the statement above would seem like an appropriately self-protective response. But where is the curiosity to explore how and why this has come about?

6) My partner does as well as she can to get her point across. However, if I don't really understand what she means, it's up to me to ask questions.

This is a very important perspective, opposite to the one expressed in the previous statement. It exemplifies a healthy self-focus in a relationship. What is missing if questions are not asked is willingness to engage.

7) My partner has a responsibility to find out whether the message he is trying to get across to me is adequate. If I understand what he says in my own way and it's different from what he intended, that's not my fault or responsibility.

This perspective centers around fault-finding and assigning blame. The focus on creating emotional safety is hard to find here. It has gone missing. Barring some extenuating circumstances that are not visible from within this statement alone, the stance sounds condescending and dismissive.

The person making the statement dismisses concern for or connection with the meaning the partner has intended to embed within the words he speaks—not a very promising sign for the relationship. This is a variation on the theme sounded in statement 5 above.

8) My partner tests me frequently. I believe she asks me to do things to exercise control or evaluate whether I care enough to do what she asks. I believe her motive is to get reassurance, but, nonetheless, I am furious that she plays games like this with me.

The person who expresses this attitude is aware that the partner is asking for reassurance. Rather than comply with her requests to perform token acts—particularly those felt to be gratuitous—can the underlying need for reassurance be addressed directly? In therapy parlance, the person's request for proof of caring is "acting out" her feeling of insecurity about the attachment. Since the message embedded in your partner's request has been decoded, if reassurance is equated with emotional nourishment, why not supply it directly? Many find it hard to ask directly for reassurance because they feel it puts them in an emotionally vulnerable position. They equate needing reassurance with feeling weak and helpless. I would want to coach people expressing this statement to give their partners the benefit of the doubt and interpret what they have been doing as their best attempt to get something that, if they could have expressed themselves more directly, would sound like a legitimate request for contact and not a form of "testing." The "testing" is a not charade but a sign of the importance of the person being asked to provide it.

The response I made in the paragraph above was based on a supposition that the testing was primarily related to seeking contact. If the underlying themes of the testing are issues like seeking control or creating distance, my recommendation would be different. In those situations, further exploration geared to tease out the destructive elements lying under the surface of these testing requests would need to be worked through.

In any case, being asked to prove continuously that you care can become tiresome. If what you are asked to do for your partner includes things she can easily do for herself, the issue of dependency becomes relevant. Perhaps she feels safe asking for contact only, or primarily under the guise of feeling dependent or even helpless. This does not mean she is doing something dishonest or wrong. Dependency is a legitimate aspect of intimate relationship. It is the flip side of reliability, which we all crave. We crave a reliable person upon whom we can depend. But as a culture, we hold dependency in low regard. We tend to see it as a weakness

That makes this issue tricky. It is a two-sided issue and there are no absolute rights or wrongs. If the dependency flows only in one direction, it is easy to understand that the person being tested would develop feelings of being treated unfairly. Those feelings deserve to be explored and worked through as well.

To the extent that there is a care-taking element in the relationship—and partners certainly do enjoy being taken care of in both healthy and not so healthy ways—we want to be careful not to be judgmental in how we respond to these requests. Having rituals of harmless dependency can sometimes build trust and help partners organize and also dispel anxieties. After all, if you can depend on someone, you are securely attached, in some respects at least. If you can rely on your partner to help you remember things you might otherwise forget, or soothe you with affection during transitions of leave-taking and homecoming or any other times, these are things that can become woven into the fabric of shared warmth and companionship. These routines can help make your relationship a refuge from the impersonality encountered outside the home.

9) My partner talks nonstop. If uninterrupted, he can go on indefinitely. Aside from not being able to get a word in edgewise, there is no room for me to develop my own perspective through a back-and-forth conversation.

Research on communication indicates that the human attention span is quite limited. We have great capacity to store memories long-term, but in the short-term, in terms of working memory, neuroscientists suggest that we hit full capacity in under a minute! From then on we absorb little. Effective communication is maximized when packaged in small chunks. Although it is difficult to pare down messages, it is important to be aware of this parameter of verbal interaction.

Small packets of language that allow partners time to metabolize what is being said before responding benefit speaker and listener. Exercising restraint by keeping messages as concise and concentrated as possible is an important and much under-acknowledged aspect of good communication.

Can you talk to your partner about leaving space in the conversation for you? Can you explain how being able to respond verbally is important to your sense of feeling connected to him or her? People who speak nonstop without leaving space for the listener may be feeling anxious about not being heard. If and when you ask them to give up the conversational floor, before launching into what you want to say, it is important that you acknowledge what they have said so that they understand they are being listened to. There are no easy answers to this problem situation. But not addressing it will likely produce so much resentment in the long run that this fragile communication process may implode.

10) Generally speaking, good communication is a matter of intelligence.

Some of the most intelligent individuals on the planet are poor communicators. Good communication has to do with being in touch with your feelings and being open to knowing and being known by your partner. Throw in a healthy dollop of motivation to make the most of life's opportunities, and you've got momentum going in the direction of good communication.

Those who wish to develop a sophisticated understanding of the communication process benefit from their knowledge, but the key is not the level of intellectual sophistication achieved, it is the willingness to engage, connect, and share openly.

11) Good communication comes from a combination of attention and emotional and cognitive skills.

I believe so. I include this item because it underscores the notion that good communication involves balance.

12) Good communication is within the grasp of any person who desires to connect with his partner.

    This perspective is true if it acknowledges that, along with a desire to connect, there must be a willingness to work on the relationship. Desire alone, without the willingness to work, is not sufficient. However, it is an important element in the process of building good communication.

13) Good communication can be foiled by too much fear and anxiety.

    I'd say so. Too much fear and anxiety turns off the reflective process as is discussed in various sections of the book—notably in the section on the limbic seesaw (see Chapter Twelve). Willingness, coupled with the intention to acknowledge difficult feelings—anxiety, for example—can help anyone to trigger the part of the brain that would ordinarily go off-line in the face of anxiety.

    A practice in which you invoke conscious questioning and acceptance of any feeling you are experiencing can help to rebalance the inner experience of fear, anxiety, anger, or any other strong emotion. With consistent practice in activating this intentionality, loss of control, in which the limbic system takes over, can be mediated.

14) Good communication makes it easier for a partner to bear her fear or anxiety.

    Two together can conquer pressures and problems to which one alone may succumb. Genuine connection makes whatever burdens you face easier to bear. The power of good communication, the bond between you and your partner, brings the promise of feeling understood and connected, of having an ally to help with every challenge you face.

15) In a good relationship it is important for both partners to say what is on their minds when they are feeling it.

It is important for partners to communicate their feelings to each other spontaneously, as long as they do so with an awareness of what is going on in the relationship and the situation in which they are expressing themselves. When I began doing couples therapy, it surprised me to find that many people believed that a good relationship required them to say what they were feeling or thinking when they were feeling or thinking it, regardless of what else was going on in the moment. They aspired to live without benefit of an emotional filter. Those who hold this principle as an ideal feel that a good relationship involves unlimited transparency of feelings and thoughts. Manny, who came to couples therapy with his partner, Audrey, said, "If I am feeling something, I want to be able to tell Audrey all about it right then and there. That's good communication. If I have to hold it in, or wait for the right time, there is something wrong with that." This concept of relationship flies in the face of some very basic and important aspects of three-dimensional communication, not to mention mindfulness.

First, good communication involves reflection on what is happening in the here and now. Any plan that builds on the right to neglect consideration of whether a particular moment would or would not be conducive to a productive talk is a road map to disconnection.

There is something to be said for spontaneous conversation. But good communication requires judicious decision making.

We cannot possibly say everything that comes into our minds; not if we have awareness of how much is going on in our minds at all times. In my opinion, making a virtue of not having a filter is a problem. Three-dimensional rule of thumb: *invite* your partner to listen. Respond to an invitation by accepting, or explain why you can't accept and then reschedule for another time. Let the ground between you be clear so that either of you can have the opportunity to reach out to make contact *without requiring* that one or the other is available, no matter what.

Whether we are talking about expressing the desire to have a conversation or to have sex or even to share a view of a sunset, respect and recognition of the sense in which your partner is entitled to feel *both* independent from *and* connected to you is important. The idea that you can say whatever you want at any time lacks this balance. It also destroys the spirit of personal freedom in a partnership. Freedom involves not only the freedom to do what you might like but also the freedom from having things done to you whenever someone else would like—regardless of how you feel about it.

Having said all of this, there is another, quite different way to look at the statement. There is great value in being in tune with your partner. Not all communication is a matter of working out differences or clarifying miscommunication or even of discovering attunement. Once you are securely attached and have confidence that you have prepared the ground for exposing more about the way you feel and think than ever before, you can move into this intimate territory. As long as you do not take your partner's availability for granted, you can reveal who you are without feeling that you are holding back. These special moments of intimate touching of mind, heart, and body can enrich, inform, enlighten, reveal, and delight. However, even under these circumstances, it pays to have respect for the fragility of relationship. Although you can share deeply and risk a deep sense of vulnerability with your partner, even at those moments you still need to maintain a sense of how your message is received. Three-dimensional communication, mindfulness, requires awareness to be the watchword, even in moments of bold self-revelation and daring.

16) A good communicator is responsible for the way his messages are received.

Communicators cannot control the way their messages are received. That depends on the listener and his stance. If the listener has preconceived ideas about what he expects to hear, it can be very difficult to get across anything outside of his expectations.

So, am I saying that the communicator has no responsibility for the way his message is received? No, and I don't want to encourage that perspective. Partners engaged in a three-dimensional communication are committed to working with each other to fortify connection. Each message represents an opportunity to strengthen it because, even if the message is not received adequately, the follow-up can bring not only repair but greater strength of connection than had existed previously. Affirmation of basic communication energizes stability and trust.

The speaker crafts a message and articulates it to the listener. Then the speaker notices whether the message has been received and, if so, wonders if it has been received in the spirit in which it was intended. This may not be possible to do in every instance, but this kind of follow-up to one's message is part of what it takes to monitor the communication process.

Should the speaker notice something that indicates the message has not been received properly, this would resonate within the third dimension of the communication process. Potentially, one or both partners would sense the incompleteness, and either the speaker would resend the message, or the listener would question his partner to understand the impasse he senses.

Mindful communication and three-dimensional communication are both forms of intentional communication.

17) People say what they mean to say. If someone makes a statement, she is responsible for the meaning of the words she said.

I include this statement because many believe that when someone says something, she means exactly what she said. Of course, this is often so. But often it is not. And not solely because people can be disingenuous.

Language itself is a complicated medium. Not everyone handles it adeptly. Academic researchers affirm that approximately 7 percent of U.S. children are diagnosed with CD (communication disorder). The problem is widespread enough to be recognized as a "major educational and public health issue." A significant number of people have great difficulty using language to capture their thoughts and feelings.

Aside from clinically identified speech and language problems, a wide discrepancy exists in the speed with which individuals process their thoughts and feelings. This differential affects greatly the flow of dialogue between partners. I have worked with many couples who felt that they were not communicating because they were unaware that the rhythm of conversation that felt natural to one partner did not feel that way to the other.

Learning to identify your partner's style of processing her thoughts and feelings—which includes converting them into language—can bolster a sense of confidence in the possibility of staying connected. Because without awareness of this discrepancy when it does exist—and it exists commonly—partners often resort to blaming and accusing each other of being too _____ (fill in the blank with one or more of these: angry, stubborn, preoccupied, disinterested, self-involved, mean, uncaring . . .) to participate in a manner that meets their expectations.

Some partners need to talk things out, to formulate their ideas out loud, and to hear their thoughts before discriminating between them and coming to awareness of what they feel or think. It is easy to see how people who can summon their thoughts, feelings, and opinions quickly and without vocalizing might be puzzled by their partners' need to go through an elaborate and interpersonal process in order to get to the same place they arrive at instantly. Such couples may feel that the partners who need additional time and effort to capture their thoughts are deliberately stalling, being oppositional, or controlling. Understanding one's thoughts is a process, and the speed with which individuals perform it varies significantly. Partners who gain knowledge of each other's language processing style often are able to sidestep significant misunderstanding and conflict.

18) Couples should represent what they feel forcefully in order to be understood. The worst flaw in couples' communication occurs when dialogue is filled with noncommittal statements.

Clarity is important. It is commendable. But it is also an achievement that often occurs after a dialogue has gone through considerable phases. It is not commonly a starting point. It is important that your dialogue with your partner include enough flexibility to allow both of you opportunities to modify your statements as you explore what you think, feel, and mean to say. Identifying thoughts and feelings, as well as recognizing changes in your own thoughts and feelings, is an ongoing process.

If you are clear about what you feel, expressing it with clarity is desirable. The variability in force is a separate matter. We think of forceful expression as being persuasive, but although it is sometimes constructive to be persuasive with your partner, generally speaking, noncompetitive sharing of thoughts and feelings—three-dimensional conversation—tends to de-emphasize the element of persuasion and replace it with encouragement and acceptance.

Sometimes the strongest communication is done with understatement. At other times, bold and direct statements are most effective. Messages need to be crafted with the current situation in mind. What does it mean if a partner expresses himself with noncommittal statements? It can mean he is unclear about what he feels or means. This may be a function of the rhythm and style with which he processes his thoughts, feelings, and language. It may also mean that he is hesitant to reveal what he thinks, in which case an exploration of why he feels hesitant would be useful. It might mean that he needs encouragement to express himself, or that he is not comfortable with the intimacy that is possible when dialogue is clearer, and because such intimacy is unfamiliar to him, it may feel scary. Intimacy in conversation is something he may have rarely experienced. It can be anxiety provoking. To sum up, the idea that partners express themselves in "noncommittal" statements can have many different meanings and is worth exploring sensitively.

19) Blurting out your feelings is always a mistake.

The tip-off here is the word *always*. Though blurting out feelings without taking notice of whether your partner is receptive or whether the moment is conducive to your being heard in the way you want to be heard can be destructive, there are times when it may be appropriate.

For example, if the issue is that one partner is suppressing or attempting to intimidate the other into silence or a subordinate position in her dialogue, it might be appropriate to make sure that you do not allow her to prevail. Here, blurting out your personal truth may be identical to claiming a place for yourself in the dialogue.

The lesson here is to maintain a healthy skepticism of any guideline that proclaims an all-or-nothing—always or never—rule in regard to interpersonal relations.

20) The longer you hold back from talking about something you feel, the more you infect your communication process with resentment.

This is an interesting and seductive proposition. More than a kernel of wisdom is contained within the statement, but ultimately it is misleading.

Let me approach it from a few vantage points. First, in many places in this book we discuss timing your communication. Timing and shaping your messages to maximize possibilities so that you feel heard is an essential aspect of three-dimensional communication. So the act of holding back can sometimes be a deliberate, effective, and compassionate choice.

We have to differentiate between the act of deliberately holding back for the sake of maximizing the effectiveness of expressing what is on your mind and the difficulty that partners may encounter in *allowing themselves* the freedom to share a feeling or idea. One is a question of deliberate timing or finesse; the other is a question of liberating oneself from inhibition. Though quite different, each is a valid concern that comes up around this issue.

The idea that the communication process becomes "infected" by resentment is an interesting one. This can happen. One partner may feel that because he is not speaking his truth and representing who he is, he is not genuinely present in the relationship. This can be oppressive and eventually spoil whatever feelings of ease and trust exist.

It is important to remember that what is being delayed is not the release of a toxic element but the commencement of the connection process. Unlike physical limitations, psychological limitations are harder for us to track and monitor. If we were told that in order to heal a long-term problem in communication, we would have to perform a superhuman task, and if that task were translated into physical terms, we could immediately gauge whether the task was doable. Or we would have a sense of how we might have to *break the task into a series of doable subtasks* to accomplish it.

The human mind is a notoriously poor judge of what it can or cannot accomplish. For example, it is important for couples to understand that if they are triggered and feel angry, they will not be able to stop on a dime and resume a reasonable conversation. It is impossible to simply "snap out of a mood" once you are biologically triggered. Yet partners often do expect themselves to continue talking long after they have become unable to listen. Translating that into physical terms might read something like this: Having a productive conversation once you/your partner are triggered is as likely as either or both of you pole vaulting over a twenty-five foot bar. The absurdity of trying to vault the twenty-five foot bar is palpable immediately. The possibility of conducting a productive conversation before calming down, equally impossible, is not perceived in the same way. This is why this method of three-dimensional communication offers partners a great opportunity to take into account how and why they will go about building a collaborative dialogue. It is tailored to the capability of the human mind, which requires consistency, and makes use of our inborn reflective capacity to integrate better means for making contact. Three-dimensional communication calls into operation the highest functionality of our biological potential, but it does not demand the impossible.

The common breakdown between partners occurs when one complains to the other, "If you loved me, you would understand how I feel without my having to explain it." This smacks of magical thinking. It also betrays a lack of under-standing of the psychological processes involved in good basic communication. *Willingness* to let go of destructive presumptions and assumptions is key to developing a three-dimensional practice.

Difficulties in communication have a long history, and transformation requires a careful and sustained effort. Of partial importance is for partners to relinquish hope for a quick fix and dedicate themselves to learning a set of prac-tices that will produce new responses to old problems. The commitment to learning is underscored. As you and your partner learn what you need to do to create emotional safety, you will notice that an atmosphere of acceptance, compassion, and encouragement emerges. There is no way to measure the potential for healing in your relationship *before* we have made a resolute attempt to create emotional safety.

Conversational Interlude 2

Hearing and Listening
What's not happening here?

Norton: Excuse me, I didn't hear you.

Olivia: That's because you aren't listening.

Norton: No, it's because you aren't saying anything.

Olivia: What I'm saying is plenty, and if you knew how to listen, you'd understand.

Norton: Well, maybe the problem is with your hearing. Because if you could hear what you were saying, you'd know it wasn't worth listening to.

Olivia: Oh, so you did hear me?

Norton: Yes. But I wasn't listening.

Olivia: At least you finally admit it.

Norton: I told you in the first place that I didn't hear you.

Olivia: But you didn't admit it was because you weren't listening.

Norton: Does that feel better now?

Olivia: Much better. At least I know whose fault it is that I'm feeling alone when we have a conversation.

Norton: You think you feel alone. If you were listening, you'd understand what alone is all about. And that's exactly the way I feel when I try to listen to you and don't hear anything.

Olivia: That's because you don't listen to what you hear.

Norton: No, that's because when I listen and hear nothing, it hurts my listening apparatus. It's like using the rug attachment of the vacuum cleaner on a bare floor. It hurts the motor, don't you know that? It's bad for the mechanism.

Olivia: Yeah, but that's the problem in the first place. You listen like a machine. Why don't you put a little heart into it? And then maybe your hearing would turn into real listening for a change.

Norton: Do you really think it would?

Olivia: I know it would.

Norton: I think you said something worth hearing there.

Olivia: Thank you.

Norton: Too bad I wasn't listening.

Olivia: Whaddya mean by that?

Norton: Well, I heard you, all right. But it's just hard to trust what I heard.

Olivia: That's the problem with listening. It involves trust. You've got to do something with what you hear, and that isn't always easy.

Norton: There you go again. There's something else that's worth hearing. This is becoming a regular thing with you.

Olivia: Thank you.

Norton: Don't thank me. Thank the part of me that listens in spite of it all. The rest of me just hears.

Olivia: Oh, so you admit it again?

Norton: Of course.

Olivia: So you admit you haven't been listening then?

Norton: If you admit you haven't heard a thing I've said, sure.

CHAPTER NINE

Learning from Mistakes

No one cares how much you know,
until they know how much you care.

—Theodore Roosevelt

Making mistakes is a price we pay for learning. Sometimes the lessons we learn penetrate to our core. A mistake can force us to acknowledge a blind spot in our outlook that needs to be taken seriously. Through committing certain kinds of mistakes, we inadvertently stumble onto a path that elevates us. This kind of learning sometimes comes about as a result of a clearly felt distinction between the circumstance in which we exist—what we think of as our normal life—and the Bizarro universe into which a mistake thrusts us. We know that we do not want to be in that Bizarro place, this alternate version of reality, imprisoned by our errors.

In this sense, making mistakes is "learning the hard way." But if we are lucky, we may get a chance to experience a reprieve. Some make a mistake and are spared its more brutal consequences. When this happens, we get a glimpse of the awesome power of an unforgiving fate without having to pay for it in full with blood, flesh, and an ocean of tears as others who have erred similarly sometimes must. Consider the following story.

Winston was the proud father of a stocky eighteen-month-old boy. The child's hair resembled yellow cotton candy, and, having recently come into his own as a fast walker, the boy strode up and down wherever he was with aggressive curiosity. He covered as much ground as quickly as possible, wherever and whenever he could. Think lion cub. The boy, Reginald, or Reggie, was visiting his favorite haunt, the Museum of Natural History, located on Eighty-First Street, in Manhattan. Winston had never been much of a museum enthusiast, but now that he was with Reginald and had absolutely no opportunity to view any of the exhibits because he was completely taken up with keeping track of Reggie, he started to feel that being in a museum and having the luxury to stop and witness the exhibits would be pure heaven. His thoughts went along these lines when he parked Reggie's stroller at the top of the stairs that led down to the Whale Room. In that cavernous space hung a replica of the eighty-three-foot blue whale, largest mammal known to man. Winston had been in the Whale Room three times within the past week and had yet to get a good look at the whale. What he had done in that space was run after Reggie, catch Reggie, feed Reggie, escort Reggie to the bathroom, and then depart from the Whale Room with Reggie in tow.

On this day, after descending the stairs, Winston planted himself in front of the sea creature and admired its girth. He noticed and remarked to himself on its outsize length. That kind of length is more than long. That's a new way of thinking about what lengthy means. And then the blueness. Indigo. Imposing as a mammoth gem, blue unlike any daylight sky, deep as blue-black velvet laid luxuriously behind and beyond a starry night. This sight was unrivaled.

When Winston looked around after his reverie, which lasted no longer than forty seconds, he sensed something awry. He glanced to the stroller. Where was Reggie? The boy had sprung loose. The first few seconds in which Winston noticed that he had indeed been a solitary observer of the whale were calm and cool enough. The thought that Reggie might be lost, had been taken, or irrecoverable had not yet occurred to him. A few seconds later the hair bristled on the back of his now clammy neck.

Then he shot into action, speeding around the museum, the gray Maclaren stroller flying before him. Assorted paraphernalia suited for contingencies like weather changes or snack time sat oddly serene where Reggie would have been had he gotten tuckered out and wanted to ride. Winston circled the perimeter of the vast space. With another forty-five seconds gone, he called Reggie's name. It was not a scream, but it had some heft to it, and it echoed through the chamber. A guard approached him. He sputtered, "My boy's gone. I don't know where he is. He was with me a minute ago. He's little, a year and a half, but he moves fast. Yellow hair, like a big puff. Did you see him?"

The guard scanned the area with his sharp eyes. "No, I didn't see him," the guard said matter-of-factly.

This set Winston on edge. How can anybody not notice something like that if it happens right in front of him? And whatever did happen must have happened right in front of him. And everybody else in the room, for that matter. *Including me*, Winston thought. That was disconcerting. The logical extension of this thought chain was that nothing could have happened. Too many people around and this was a safe place. Winston wanted to believe in this safety, but he didn't see Reggie, so *something* must have happened. Otherwise Reggie would be right by his side.

Winston's teeth had begun to chatter ever so slightly. He balled his hand into a fist and squatted so he could survey the room at floor level like a landscaper or a bomb squad specialist peering under cars. That didn't help. He would never be able to explain this to his wife. How could he?

But where was Reggie? Was he with someone who would hurt him? Winston felt like he was in a falling elevator whose cable had been cut. He knew what plummeting felt like. Still, he made an effort to stay composed, tried not to allow the slow trotting panic to burst into a full gallop. He called out in a louder voice, "Reggie! Where are you? Reggie!"

A second guard moved toward him. Approximately three minutes had passed by then. Enough time had elapsed so that Reggie might conceivably be caught on some security camera approaching an exit. Some degenerate, probably a man, might be pictured there, scooping Reggie into his arms as they half walked, half ran toward a parked car. Winston's head was exploding. He was in the Bizarro universe, and he would have paid any price to be returned to the world of just a few minutes before. Four minutes and counting. The portal that would lead him back into what he thought of as a normal reality was receding. It seemed that the world in which something dreadful occurred at the museum was filling in with unwanted detail.

The first security guard returned and waved Winston toward him. Winston moved in the guard's direction. As if directing the delicate parking procedure of a large truck into a small space, the guard placed both hands by his ears and was wagging his middle fingers, thumbs held steady, vigorously toward his face, the signal for directing a driver to keep the vehicle moving.

The feeling that nothing in his life would ever be the same again consumed Winston. It was over five minutes now since he had last seen Reggie. Fate had been cast to the wind. The guard had switched up and was giving him a windmill motion with his right arm, circling vigorously from the spot where he stood far across the room under the shadow of the great blue monstrous tail.

Winston ran toward the guard, carrying the stroller chest high. When he got to the guard, he spotted a structural beam just beyond the corner of the room. From there he saw an alcove with three benches, each facing the other and forming an enclosure. In the middle of the space Reggie was climbing onto one seat and then back down and then back up onto another seat. Winston quickly relocated the portal that had ushered him into that Bizarro universe in which parents hunt everywhere for lost children who are never found. He closed his eyes. He felt like reprimanding Reggie but instead hugged him tight. The hug was too strong, it could have crushed the little gurgling thing. Winston released his grip as if a jolt of high-voltage power had stung his muscles into relaxing instantaneously. Winston turned to the guard and thanked him profusely.

When Winston described the experience, he told me that it had permanently reset the standard of caution he exercised when caring for Reginald and later his daughter, Bea. Forty or so seconds can make the difference between having a child by your side and having your child wander into the unknown. He determined never to give up those forty seconds to anything ever again. This mistake taught him how to incorporate a zero tolerance for sloppy caregiving. The new standards for diligence in maintaining awareness of his children's whereabouts would previously have felt excessive to him. He now felt they were imperative and unquestionable.

Winston was not a religious person, but he felt blessed to have learned this lesson without paying a greater price. He had gotten his life back. In those brief moments in that alternate reality, he had seen his marriage disintegrate, and he now saw and felt it restored to him. He had seen the arc of his life story crash and then hoist back into place. How would he tell his wife about this? Would he tell his wife about this? He would. But first he needed to recover.

Because much of learning is trial and error, making mistakes is unavoidable. We do not tell the world who we are; through experience, the world helps us understand the shape of our identity and its deeper parameters. This is one of the key ways we learn about parenting, though hopefully not the only way. The same can be said about the way we learn to love and the way we learn about the meaning of love. We do not and cannot know exactly what we need to know until we learn what that is. Often that learning involves something obvious, like how and why forty seconds of staring at a great blue whale can cost years of suffering and torment. The same holds for any number of things: the knowledge we need to protect our children, control our anger, monitor our attention, live up to our agreements, and convey love to our partners so they feel it.

Each change or phase of identity in the life of a couple brings new sensitivities, challenges, and considerations. What we focus on in terms of desires and also accomplishments changes. Staying intimately connected with our partners requires that we keep developing skills and awareness: Old insights, crisp and relevant at one time, can become stale. One of these skill areas has to do with creating a culture within our relationships that allows us to redeem the value and learning inherent in productive mistakes. Perfectionism, the wish to hold your relationship to a mistake-free standard, inflicts a pressure that weakens your development and humanity as a couple. Albert Einstein said, "Anyone who has never made a mistake has never tried anything new." I like the quote because it underscores that there is something to be said for keeping a *positive* accounting of mistake making. At the beginning of therapy, partners often want to know how to correct mistakes. That's fine; only, in order to correct some crucial mistakes, what's necessary is not to avoid them but to transform them into the lessons that are embedded within the experience of having made them.

In this next vignette, a person felt that the particular mistake he made, although it endangered him, laid the foundation for a tremendous breakthrough in his understanding of himself and his relationship with his wife.

Jeffrey's cottage stood by the lake. He'd left in a distracted state of mind. He had just finished discussing his money situation with Alana, his wife of fifteen years. They were going to have to tighten their belts and forego numerous planned activities in the coming year in order to pay their bills. Those changes were painful enough, but Alana pinned the blame for their financial downturn squarely on Jeffrey's shoulders. Yes, he acknowledged that he had done his share and had spent unwisely at times. He admitted that he deserved to be called out for what he hadn't done well, but the way she spoke to him in anger rubbed him the wrong way. *Is that how you talk to someone you love? Even if I made mistakes, I don't deserve to be spoken to like that. When everything is going well, she's good to me. That's great, but now that we are having trouble, that's when I need her to be good to me even more.* He wrestled with these thoughts as he hopped into his car, turned the ignition, and rolled toward the state highway.

He turned right then left and saw Fern Lake disappear from his rearview mirror. The car ambled along the hilly, curving road toward Leicester Square, passing the Saturday morning signs announcing yard sales and an upcoming church dinner. When he came to the main thoroughfare in this part of central western Vermont, where a general store stood at one point of the four-corner intersection, he stopped momentarily. Then, without signaling, he pulled out onto the two-lane blacktop. He gunned the motor and shot across the northbound lane to the southbound. With the nose of the car out in the middle of the lane, Jeffrey noticed a black Subaru station wagon barreling straight at him. He instinctively floored the gas pedal and zoomed across in a wide arc. The driver of the Subaru had no time to slow down, and the shoulders on the road were slender. The other driver swerved slightly, inches really, and blared his horn. Jeffrey felt a swoosh of wind come off the Subaru as it whizzed by. Though this took place in a matter of a few seconds, Jeffrey experienced it as if in slow motion. When the black car had passed, normal time resumed. If the scene had been caught on camera, it would have seemed a daredevil stunt executed with sufficient split-second timing to make an audience swoon before offering a standing ovation. Viewers would have marveled that two cars could come that close to colliding without causing so much as a scratch. That they did not make any contact made the moment feel all the more dreamlike to Jeffrey, who was soaked in sweat. He pushed on and made his way down the now empty road toward sleepy Brandon township.

He had jumped into the car to distance himself from the feeling he was experiencing in the cottage with Alana. He had no idea where he was going at first, but he wanted to get away from the thoughts that were consuming him, thoughts of his own ineptitude and anger at Alana for lacing into him when he was already hurting. He felt unappreciated and angry.

What mistakes had Jeffrey made? The glaringly obvious one is that he pulled his car out into traffic without looking. But why? How did it happen? Instead of processing his emotions consciously, he was doing his best to get away from them, trying not to be aware of them. By numbing awareness of his feelings—the technical term would be *dissociating*—he also dulled himself to his surroundings.

The connection between avoiding feelings and putting yourself in harm's way is clear in this vignette. People do this with driving, they do it with drinking and drugs, and they do it in many other ways. Seeking relief from anxiety and anger is natural, but we pay an enormous price if we sacrifice mindful processing of emotion to the wish for escape. It's not like Jeffrey consciously decided on this strategy. In fact, he had no conscious awareness of it. He was so angry, he was willing to hurl his future into oblivion, not to mention the future of the family riding along in the Subaru.

Jeffrey sped down the road until he got to Brandon, a quaint locale north of Rutland. There he parked and sat in the car. He described the experience to me in this way: "I don't know if I was thinking in words right then. But in any case, what I realized was that I had put my entire life in jeopardy. In that one moment I could have lost the opportunity to see my daughters grow up. Some trade-off! I could easily have been killed or put myself in a wheelchair for life. However I think about how or why it happened, I realize that I have a second chance to live my life. I felt a great sadness. I was thinking about how lucky I was and then about all the thousands or maybe even millions of others who had been careless in their cars for a matter of seconds and paid for it so much more tragically. I was very lucky, considering. I had gotten into my car feeling upset and tried to cool off by going for a spin. I was an idiot."

Jeffrey took a sip of water and continued. "My answer to feeling bad was to run away. I can't do that anymore. And I can't run away from how I feel because this is what happens. I was lucky this once, but chances are that if this happened again, I wouldn't get out of it without a lot of pain. I don't have to get into a metal-on-metal car accident to get the message. It's dangerous for me to run away from my feelings. I can't drive either my car or my life without paying attention to what I'm doing. I can't do that. Not if I want to feel good about my life.

"From that day on, I even changed my way of handling money. I was moving ahead in situations, like I did in the car, without looking first or figuring out what would be best for me and my family, and for me and my wife. My wife was more sympathetic and understanding when she realized that I had made changes. Not just talked about making them, but made them. She started to believe in me again. That anger I had heard in her voice, that's not what really bothered me, I know that now. What really bothered me was that I knew that she had lost faith in me. And I can understand why. And it wasn't just for her own sake that she was reacting. I was falling down as a father and letting our money situation get dragged down. That mistake woke me up, maybe like nothing else could have. It sounds crazy to say, but that mistake was one of the greatest experiences I've ever had."

I wouldn't wish Jeffrey's mistake on anyone because with the mistake would come the risk that things would not turn out as well. But it's easy to understand what he means when he says that the mistake was one of the luckiest things that ever happened to him. It enabled him to see himself differently and form the necessary resolve to take action. A blind spot in his perspective about who he was became visible to him.

Why do I choose an example like this to discuss mistake making in a book about couples? Because the way we handle our feelings as individuals and the mistakes we make in processing our emotions have a profound influence on the way we function as partners in relationships. A good relationship dynamic sustains and nourishes us so that we can face challenges within and outside the relationship. An internal dynamic that blocks mindfulness and the habit of running away from awareness of feelings is dangerous for individuals and relationships.

Most people tell me that they want to avoid repeating past mistakes. Few ever say that they want to hold on to what they've learned from their mistakes—they simply don't want to make them again. I am trying to promote the need for us all to open up *that* category—what we learn from mistakes—as important and worth affirming.

Learning to love is an extended process, and, fortunately or not, most of us enter long-term relationships with preconceptions and misconceptions that get in the way of knowing and being known by our partners. To free ourselves from the constrictions imposed by these pre- and misconceptions, we have to accept that mistakes are inevitable and that some will open doors to deeper contact with our partners and with ourselves.

I want to review some large mistakes that plague many relationships and see if I can put them in a context that will be helpful for anyone who is looking to work as productively as possible with mistakes. Let's hold that in mind as we consider Jerard's situation.

Jerard knew he was making a certain kind of mistake frequently. He knew it was damaging his relationship with his wife, but he had no confidence in his ability to do otherwise. He stands out in my memory as a person who demonstrated perseverance in sorting out what it would take to make necessary changes. He had great awareness and insight into how he functioned in his relationship with his wife. His problem lay in acting as if he hadn't any. The link between what he knew and what he was able to modify in his behavior was broken.

Some back story: Jerard had a way with a certain kind of storytelling. He had parlayed it into a career, and, although he never gained prominence with the public, it won him a niche audience and a comfortable living. He wrote stories about the lives of small-time players in positions of limited power in and around New York City. Like numerous other Jewish American writers, he was fascinated with the city. Its glamour, grandeur, and guttural qualities were his true subject. He chiseled his fictitious characters out of experience with relatives, neighborhood characters, and family friends.

On this morning as he walked into the living room and greeted his wife, Lori, a kindergarten teacher for the past fifteen years, she was busy wrestling with plans for a gut renovation of their second bathroom. After a quick breakfast of toast and coffee for both, she explained that she had errands to run and needed to take the car. They had two cars, but the Toyota was in the shop, so each was relying on a late model Chevy and took turns using it. As Lori was leaving the apartment she said, "I'll have the car back by two. By then Anita may be here. Could you wash up the dishes and straighten up the living room so I won't have to do it when I get back? Would you do that for me, honey?"

Jerard heard the words through a haze. Or maybe it would be more accurate to say he heard indistinct sounds that could have been words. He was thinking about a scenario in which the protagonist of his latest narrative, Charles Gerson, came to terms with the fact that no matter how high up he rose in what was once called the *schmatta* business, he would never win the respect and recognition from his siblings that had been heaped on his older brother. The one and only Larry Gerson was the family success story, a Wall Street wunderkind whose uncanny talent with numbers bordered on the supernatural. Charles had risen from retail sales to managing a number of Florsheim outlets before working his way up to being top salesman at a reputable Fashion Avenue firm. But he would never make the kind of money that Larry raked in. Charles comforted himself with the knowledge, "At least I know who I am. Larry lives in a cloud of line graphs and algorithms."

Jerard stepped toward the table, brushed off some toast crumbs, made a fresh cup of coffee, and began pecking away at his laptop computer. Charles had not only announced his presence but was opening up to Jerard. He wanted to be there and take full advantage of the opportunity. Such things do not always come a second time.

Before he knew it, the door swung open and Lori sang out, "Made it back. I cut my day short to make sure you'd have a car by two in case you need it."

Jerard smiled without looking up from his computer screen. He pursed his lips and furrowed his brow. "Thanks. Hey, what do you mean? I don't need the car."

Lori looked around and noticed the dishes in the sink and disorder in the living room. Then she reacted as if she had been struck between the eyes with a dart. Her face reddened. She put her right hand to her forehead. "You could have said you weren't going to straighten up when I asked you. You know I don't ask you for much."

"I'm sorry. I had intended to take a few minutes and wash the dishes, but I didn't get to it. I was distracted," Jerard said.

"Did you hear me ask you to help me out?" She began to cry and made choking sounds. "You know, either you don't listen to me because you don't think I'm important enough to listen to, or you listen but don't think I'm important enough to deserve a response. Either way, I'm tired of being treated like I'm nothing." She looked past him at the kitchen and her face grew stern. "I'm not going to put up with being treated this way."

Jerard felt a surge of anger within himself but tempered it. Whether she was right or not, he didn't like to be criticized. But he knew she was right. He had felt a response like this had been brewing in Lori for a while and that it was inevitable. He knew that he had been distracted lately and hardly paid attention to her. He nodded his head when she talked to him but often had no idea what she was saying because he didn't listen much. Then when he did tune in, if she said something he disagreed with, he would be sure either to tell her why he thought what she was saying was wrong or simply make a face. She had told him about those faces. She let him know, "They are worse than your know-it-all opinions."

He told me that through all of it, he honestly didn't understand why he treated her this way. He acknowledged that she was intelligent, kindhearted, and good-natured. He described it to me like this: "I'm in a good marriage. But do you wanna know what's wrong with it? It's the way I treat my wife." He asked if I could help him to do better.

On the day she returned to the unwashed dishes, he said to her, "I am sorry. You are important to me. And you are right. You deserve more from me." He meant what he said but had little confidence he could deliver "more" because he didn't understand why he wasn't delivering it already.

She slumped into a brown easy chair. "You don't act like you feel that way. The way you act makes me feel alone. There were a number of other things I wanted to take care of. Instead of doing them, relaxing and taking care of what I needed to do, I had my eye on the clock the whole time and hurried back because I thought you might need the car. Then to walk in and realize that, as usual, I was thinking of you but you didn't give me a second thought. There's ten minutes of straightening up to do here, and it's mostly your things that are strewn around. Half of the dishes are yours. I wasn't asking for anything extraordinary, just some ordinary cooperation."

"I had no idea you thought I needed a car today. I never told you that," Jerard mumbled.

"Okay. You never told me that. So I made a mistake in what I remembered. But I asked you for a simple favor, and if you weren't going to do it, I'd have come back even earlier. Was I talking to a wall? What about thinking about what I say? This voice that I use, it's not a disembodied spirit. It's not a ventriloquist speaking through me. I wasn't acting as a medium channeling somebody else's request. The things I asked you to do, I asked because I wanted them done. Me. Remember me? We live together. If I ask you to help me out and it's easy for you to do what I'm asking, I expect you to come through for me. Because when you don't, I feel like a fool for coming through for you. Or at the very least, tell me that you're not going to do what I ask. Is that really too much to expect?"

"No," Jerard said. "I should have said something at the least. I can't tell you why I didn't. I wish I had. I'm sorry."

"If this was a rare occurrence, I'd take it and your apology in stride. It wouldn't be any big deal. We all make mistakes. I do too. But I feel mistreated," Lori said. She got on the phone and called Anita, who hadn't left her house yet. She asked her if they could get together an hour later than planned. She turned back to Jerard. "I need some time by myself right now."

Jerard left the apartment to give her space. Since the car was back, he went for a drive. As he approached the West Side Highway, it occurred to him that his thinking was strange. It felt almost like he wasn't driving the car himself. He noticed that his arms were steering the car as if he were observing himself on automatic pilot. He steered the vehicle parallel to the other cars that were turning right and heading uptown. The car moved steadily, as it might on any normal day, within the flow of cars beside him. He noticed the brackish water of the Hudson. He shook his head in an effort to get himself to focus on the road in front of him. It frightened him to feel that he didn't know what was going on inside his own mind. He recalled a time when he had realized that his relationship to his first wife was irreparably damaged. He recalled how depressed he was at that time. He hadn't felt that way for a long time, but now he was feeling something similar.

He rode along mindlessly, like a leaf on a stream of rainwater, until he found himself at 181st Street. He exited there, parked the car, and traipsed toward a coffee shop he had frequented years ago, when he'd first started seeing Lori. He entered the coffee shop and sat in an empty booth opposite the cash register, facing a plate glass window that looked out on Broadway near the George Washington Bridge. The place had not changed much, although he no longer recognized any of the staff. He ordered a cup of coffee and a pastry and stared at the window. An observer may have assumed he was watching passersby or perhaps waiting for someone to meet him, but his eyes were trained on the reflection of his face in the glass. He sipped black coffee. From time to time, he nibbled the flaky cherry danish. For nearly an hour he sat studying the expression on his face, thinking about what Lori had said. He looked hard, as if to discern some secret embedded within his facial expression. He held a conviction, born of the moment, that something was there, something others were able to decode but which eluded him. He looked hard and deep and long, hoping to see what he felt others could take in at a glance. But nothing came clear.

When he rose from the table and paid the bill, he still felt shaken. He was going to get to the bottom of what was going on with him and maybe with Lori. He was going to make it his business to do something.

That was the incident that brought them in for couples therapy.

Up to this point, Jerard had felt that the only thing he could do to preserve his place in the relationship was to continue to hide the fact that he was emotionally absent much of the time. This was a big mistake. Although it may seem elementary, this is a common error in relationships. Posed in relation to an ongoing problem, the question often gets voiced internally like this: "I realize that something is going wrong. Should I hide it for as long as possible, until I am discovered? Or should I take the bull by the horns, bring it up, and see if I can engage my partner in helping me work with it?" Partners wait far too long before they take their difficulties with communication seriously enough to resolve to address them.

It's easy to see why partners make this mistake. It's hard to make yourself vulnerable and own up to a pattern you don't feel good about. It can feel like you are relinquishing control when you acknowledge and take responsibility for a problem. Acknowledging that you have a problem by fessing up to it makes you feel you've lost control of it as a private concern, as a secret. It can be helpful to hold in mind that at the same time you seem to lose control of the situation by "letting the secret out," you simultaneously gain control as you actively address the problem you are acknowledging. Taking responsibility releases you from feeling powerless to do anything about the situation because talking about it and trying to work it out constitute doing something about it.

Trepidation about the possibility that help will be forthcoming and doubts about whether things can improve are other obstacles holding back partners from dealing with issues that interfere with their ability to connect. Facing problems does take courage. But keep in mind that the longer partners wait, the more ingrained problems become. The trepidation does not dissipate with inactivity; to the contrary, the longer it is ignored, the harder it becomes to deal with.

Active commitment to noticing whether emotional safety is being strengthened or weakened by what is unfolding in the here and now makes the third dimension come alive. That, in itself, signifies being in active mode with reflective capacities online.

Still, I have yet to hear a couple come in for couples counseling and report, "The problem we are having is that we are both passive when it comes to creating emotional safety." The closest I have heard, and I consider this to be a hopeful prognostic indicator, is, "We want to learn how to do better. Our communication breaks down and we want to understand what we can do to make that happen less or not at all." This statement indicates that the couple is already in active mode.

Back to Jerard: Until the epiphany in the coffee shop, he was operating with a passive strategy. He realized that he could not avoid Lori becoming aware that he was not participating fully in the relationship. Yet he felt, "If I share what I am going through with her, she will become even more enraged with me. I'm trapped. Damned if I do, damned if I don't."

When you are in an interpersonal dilemma and find yourself think-ing that you have no reasonable option, it is usually a mistake to con-clude that you are thinking clearly. Feeling trapped tends to generate fatalistic and pessimistic strategies. Ideas that help to discover pos-sibilities for making things better come from being able to envision the possibility of things getting better. Pessimism works against this happening. So how can we deal with this pessimism? Here is my advice: consider the feeling of "trapped-ness" as a signal that the time to figure out how best to respond to the problem at hand has come. "Feeling trapped" does not mean that your options have disappeared, but that the time for heightened focus on crafting a solution has come. Reframe a "damned if you do or don't" feeling to mean that not-doing is no longer tenable.

Solving a problem involves taking a chance on implementing a strategy, often one that hasn't been tried before. Three-dimensional communication is just such a strategy. Consciously attempting to implement an assertive course of action helps you think more optimis-tically. In itself, this is an excellent way to generate creative possibilities.

As we worked together, Lori became aware of how upset Jerard felt after disappointing her by not helping her around the house. She heard him accept responsibility for a substantial share of the nega-tive pattern in their communication. She responded in a much more accepting and compassionate manner than he had anticipated. When she heard that he believed he had invested a lot in their marriage and was furious with himself for damaging it through thoughtlessness, carelessness, and preoccupation, she was moved. She felt for him, again in ways he had not expected. He had anticipated little more than anger. In the end, his ability to feel his feelings, share them openly with Lori, and speak with conviction about wanting to do better all aided in the healing process.

CHAPTER TEN

Two Gigantic Pitfalls

*It's hard to practice compassion when
we're struggling with our authenticity or
when our own worthiness is off-balance.*
—Brene Brown

We are subject to their influence, yet many do not know what they are. They are all-pervasive, but many of us do not see them anywhere. These forces are *as universal as gravity.* As my sister-in-law, Laura, used to say, "You may not like it, but it's the law." In other words, we are affected by these forces whether we want to be or not, whether we are aware of them or not. They influence how we think and feel and perceive our life situations. They affect how we process what we perceive. They cause certain matters to feel weighty, and others that we ought to take seriously float away from notice.

Two Pitfalls So Big They Are Easy to Fall Into

What forces am I talking about? The power of the unconscious is the first; we tend to deny its influence on our relationships and pay a price for that. Second is the extent to which our preconceptions limit our ability to clearly see what is in front of our noses.

As a culture we have a gross prejudice against acknowledging the power of the unconscious. We prefer to think that a relationship with problems is defective, rather than acknowledge that relationships are complex and require work—in part because they involve unconscious elements. We come to relationships with a consumer mentality. If the relationship doesn't work well, plug and play right out of the box, user-friendly, and able to withstand mistreatment without breaking down, we are dissatisfied. If these criteria are not met, we move on to thinking of the setup, the product or relationship, as replaceable/expendable/interchangeable.

The media publicizes myths that glamorize and romanticize as they caricature and dehumanize the essence of adult love relationships. The accoutrements of fame and wealth rather than soulfulness are trumpeted throughout, despite the surge of neuroscientific as well as psychological evidence that shows that each of us, and each of our relationships, has idiosyncratic needs and qualities that cannot be reduced to prevailing stereotypes.

The second large idea is related but, in some respects, opposite to the first. It has to do not so much with not knowing what is on our minds but more with having an idea, a preconception that distracts us. We could call it a *mind-set* or a way of seeing things. As a result we do not notice important goings-on around us unless they fall in line with our preoccupations.

Said simply, we see and deal with what we expect to see and deal with and, to a very significant degree, are oblivious to vital information we do not expect to encounter. Our ability to see, organize, recognize, identify, or understand important elements in our life situations is affected *because* we have consciously or unconsciously fixed our focus on *something else*.

When I began my career as a therapist almost thirty years ago, many of my clients were teenagers. Concerning the unconscious, I'd like to illustrate the first principle by describing the work I did with Arturo. He was fourteen years of age, lanky, and handsome when I met him at the outpatient mental health clinic, now affiliated with Bronx Lebanon Hospital on the Grand Concourse near Fordham Road. He was soft-spoken and well-mannered in my office; however, the notes on his chart informed me that he had been disrespectful to teachers. The guidance counselor at his school gave his mother a choice: take him for counseling, or the school would expel him. His behavioral difficulties coincided with his parents' separation. His father had moved back to Puerto Rico, and Arturo had not seen him in over eighteen months.

Arturo was punctual to sessions and seemed to enjoy them. We started off playing board and card games with sparse conversation. He tended to respond with single syllables at first. Gradually we switched over to having extended conversation in the foreground and games as a backdrop. Arturo wanted me to know about his friends, about his ever-changing cavalcade of "mad cute" girlfriends, about certain teachers who he said "didn't like" him, and about problems that sometimes came up with his mother and brother. His behavior at school had improved somewhat since he'd been coming in for counseling, but a new problem pattern had begun. He spoke rudely to his mother and was less cooperative around the house.

His mother asked for help developing strategies to support and understand him better. She asked, "Why does he treat me the way he does? I am always trying to help, and he knows that I love him. It's not fair. And I don't want him growing up to be like his father. His father doesn't treat women very well."

When I met with Arturo, I did what I could to carry these concerns forward.

He was surprised to hear that his mother thought he was angry with her. "I'm not angry with her. That's crazy, no way." We reviewed some of the situations that had developed in the home. I asked him to think one particular situation through with me.

I said, "This is what your mom told me. I'm going to describe the situation the way I understand things were last Monday. After I'm finished, tell me if it's the way you remember it. If there are any differences between what you think happened and what I am saying, please let me know about that. Is that okay with you?"

"Okay."

"Your mom said that you came home about two hours late. According to her, she had asked you to be home by 5:30 for dinner. You came home at 7:30. She told me that when she asked you why you were late, you said, 'That's none of your business. I'm here now.' Then she told you that she had prepared chicken and rice for you and that you said, 'Why did you make that again? Don't you know how to make something else?' She told me that she made that dish because that's something she knew you'd like. So far, Arturo, does this seem right to you?"

"Yeah. It's right. But I wasn't mad at her. I just didn't feel like having that food. Just because I come home late? That doesn't mean I'm angry. I wasn't mad with her. She's my mom. I love my mom. I am not mad with my mom."

"And if you love somebody, you can't be mad with them?" I asked.

"I don't know, but if I was mad at her, I would know it, right?"

"You know, Arturo, you are amazing. That is the exact question I was hoping you would ask me. Because it's something I wanted to talk to you about, but I didn't know if you would be interested in hearing about it."

"About what?"

"About the fact that it is possible to be mad with somebody and not even know it. Not even be aware of it," I said.

"What? That's crazy."

"Do you think so?"

"Yeah," he said. "That's real crazy."

"Okay. A lot of people think that their minds can't work like that, but one of the things you learn in counseling is that all of our minds— my mind too—can work just like that. People can feel something and not be aware that they feel it."

"Then how can you know you feel that way if you don't know it when it's happening?"

"You ask the greatest questions, you really do. And I'm going to give you my best answer. You may agree with me and maybe not. I want you to tell me what you think. You asked me how you can know you have a feeling if you are not feeling it, right? Here is my answer to your question: Sometimes, instead of asking yourself whether you feel angry, you think about things that you are doing or that you have done. And you think about what the things that you do might mean. So, for example, let's say we weren't even talking about you. Let's say we were talking about some guy that you know."

"All right."

"And his mother is home with his sister." I said. "His mom said that she wants him home at 5:30, and he knows that she will have it on her mind if he is late. He knows that if he is ten minutes late she will not worry too much. Twenty minutes late, she probably wouldn't worry too much either. At forty-five minutes late, she is starting to worry. It's starting to bother her because she is thinking that maybe something is wrong. And this guy has an idea that this is going on. An hour and fifteen minutes and she's really worried. She feels like going out and looking for him, but she can't leave the apartment because the little sister is there, eating dinner and then has to get ready for bed. After two hours, the guy shows up. His mother is really upset by then. She's been worrying. She asks him where he's been. Now, let's say he answers her in a polite way because he knows that she's been worried about him. If he did that you might say that he is showing concern for his mom. Would you say that?"

"I guess so."

"And if he said, 'None of your business, I'm here now.' What does that say about his concern for what his mom might be feeling? Because remember, he knows his mother, and he knows that she would be worried if he was two hours late." I stopped talking to see how Arturo would respond.

"I don't know," he said.

"Okay, let's talk about you and your mom. You knew that your mom wanted you home at 5:30. If you had come home a few minutes late, do you think she would have minded?"

"Nah."

"But after a half hour or more, she probably would be worried, right?"

"Maybe."

"So when you were two hours late, you knew she would be worried, right?"

"Yeah, but I didn't think about it."

"Well, that's what I mean about not knowing what you were feeling. You knew she'd be worried because you know her, just like the guy in the story I was telling you knew his mom. Somewhere in your mind you knew she'd be worried, but you weren't thinking about something you knew. If you are walking down the street and you are not thinking that two plus two equals four, it doesn't mean you don't know it while you are walking down the street, right? It just means you aren't thinking about it right then. Right?"

"I guess."

"So somewhere in your mind, but not in the thoughts you were having, you also knew that your mom was worrying about you, that coming home two hours late was going to be upsetting for her. Right?"

"Yeah."

"So if you upset someone, and you know you are going to upset them, usually that's the way you act when you're angry at someone. But you weren't thinking you were angry, but the way I'm talking about it, it sounds like you might have been angry but not been aware of it."

"Maybe, but I never heard of that before," he said.

"And when she asked you why you were late, you had a chance to say something friendly or polite, but instead you said something unfriendly, like, 'It's none of your business.'" I paused before continuing. "Why do you think she was worried when you were late?"

"Because she's my mom, and she cares about me."

"So what do you feel when I tell you that when you said to her that it was 'None of your business,' she told me that it hurt her feelings. Can you understand that? In fact she said that she didn't deserve to be spoken to that way. Does that make sense to you?"

"Kind of."

"Can you understand that she felt that you were angry at her because, otherwise, she told me, 'Why wouldn't Arturo just say why he was late?' Or even say that you were sorry for being late?"

"Okay. That would have been better. That was my bad. It was her business because she's my mom, but I still wasn't angry."

"Okay. So you were late enough to make her worry, and then when she asked you about it, you acted like she didn't have a right to ask you."

"I guess."

"You say you weren't mad; does what you said sound friendly?"

He shook his head.

"And then when she told you what she had made for dinner, it was something that she knows that you like, right?"

"Yeah, usually," he said.

"So somewhere in your mind you probably knew that she had made it for you?"

"Maybe. But I can say whatever I want. She's my mom."

"Sure you can. Nobody can control the muscles in your mouth, but you can also hurt people's feelings with things you say. And in this case, she is saying that you did."

"Yeah."

"And what I'm saying is that when you say, 'She's my mom, and I can say what I want,' it's like you are saying something and leaving out a part of what you are saying."

"What do you mean?"

"I mean that you are saying out loud, 'She's my mom, and I can say what I want' and that means the same thing as, 'She's my mom, and I can say what I want, even if it hurts her feelings.' And if you have no concern for her feelings, that sounds kind of angry to me. What do you think?"

"Maybe," he said. "Maybe, but I didn't really mean to hurt her feelings. I just wanted to say whatever."

"Well, now you have a chance to understand that 'whatever' sometimes means that you are either angry or acting like you are angry. Or, at the very least, acting like you don't really care if you hurt somebody's feelings."

"Whoa! What are you trying to do?"

"This thing that we are talking about today is something that a lot of grown-ups don't understand. I'm trying to help you see that feelings can be complicated. That you can have more than one feeling at the same time. And that you can sometimes be aware of some thoughts or feelings you have and unaware of others. That's what we started out talking about. Sometimes you have to talk about feelings with somebody in order to understand them.

"One last thing. Instead of feeling something, there are times when a person will do something to express the feeling that they don't even know they have. That's called being out of touch with what you are feeling. And that is the way a lot of people hurt other people's feelings. We can talk about this again another time. It's a lot. You may have questions about it."

Arturo looked me in the eye. "*Hmm*. All right. I will think about it."

"And while you think about it, let me make a suggestion," I said.

"What's that?"

"If you follow what I was saying, I'm not saying you're bad because of what you did. That's not my point. And I don't want you to feel bad. But I'm saying that the way I understand it now, and maybe you understand it this way too, you did something and it ended up hurting your mom's feelings. You are clear that you didn't want to hurt her feelings, right?"

"Yeah, that's right," he said.

"What do you think about this idea: since you hurt your mom's feelings and you didn't mean to, what do you think you might want to do about that?"

"What?"

I raised my eyebrows. "Guess."

He smiled. "Say sorry."

"What do you think about that?"

"Maybe," he said.

"How would you feel doing that?"

"Probably all right."

Talking to a teenager about the difference between the feelings their actions express and how that might not be identical to the feelings they are aware of in the moment is an objective in working with them. Anything that helps them identify, label, and ultimately regulate their feelings can be helpful to them. But the lesson is applicable to us all. When we are angry, we tend to feel entitled and empowered by our anger, and we can often act impulsively *without regard for the object of our anger.* That can become a pattern that erodes trust and makes healing more difficult the longer it goes on.

If we believe that there is no such thing as having a feeling without being aware of it—which is a way of stating that there is no such thing as the unconscious, that all the contents of your mind are always available to your awareness—and if we dismiss the distinction between feelings we are aware of and feelings that we are responsible for, we will not be able to figure out our motivation in numerous important situations. As a result, we hamstring our efforts to create emotional safety.

Just for the record, I was not entirely convinced back then that Arturo was angry with his mother. I was convinced he was angry at something or someone, and that he was unaware of his anger. Perhaps he was displacing anger at his father onto his mother? Or was angry at his younger sister for displacing him as the unrivaled focus of his mother's parental attention? However, the idea was for me to help him to become aware of his feelings and to be accountable for them, regardless of what the true source of the anger was—assuming the anger was unconscious, that he really did not understand where it was coming from. Anger is usually multidetermined anyway; it comes from many different sources within. Nonetheless, he had to learn to be accountable for his feelings and to understand himself as well as possible.

Arturo found it quizzical, amusing at first, when I spoke to him about having a feeling and not being aware of what it was. It contradicted his notion of common sense. That's understandable. Although he may have grasped the idea in part, I was seeding his understanding of the notion. It takes us all a while before we integrate it, and even then this idea never loses a certain sense of strangeness because its power resides in acknowledging that we often have no idea about realities that are emanating from within ourselves. An uncomfortable notion. The concept of the unconscious leads us toward understanding that we have a reflective capacity and can utilize it to discriminate between the meaning of what we say and what we do; they are not always identical. The discrepancy between the two is sometimes invisible to us. The relationship between what we know and what we do not know that we know is also part of this domain.

These are sophisticated notions. At least at first, many of the couples I work with are highly resistant to the idea that the mind might work this way. Or they feel that even if it does work this way, it is impossible to take these factors into account when making decisions and thinking about what is "really" important.

Many feel that it is imperative for us all to deal with the cut-and-dried, what we can see, feel, taste, and touch before us. We need to deal with what is in front of us. That is imperative. I agree. But dealing with what we see, feel, taste, and touch involves utilizing what we know. And the realm of knowing, of judgment, of how we know what we know, involves layers of understanding that include unconscious elements.

In other words, to deal with what is set before us in our life situations, we must also deal with what has come before that situation took the form in which it now can be recognized. The history of how and why we understand things as we do and how we relate to things as we do is significant. To understand how to build what we want and need, we must understand much about what we have, about what we are attempting to transform. We must be mindful.

The unconscious does not in itself introduce complications into the way we view relationship; it gives us a way to speak about those complications. The complications are there anyway. Although the notion of having unconscious thoughts and feelings is not new and is utilized by professionals all the time, it has yet to penetrate deeply into mainstream American thinking.

Many couples attempt to close themselves off to the idea that their judgments or perspectives might be affected by thoughts and feelings they harbor but do not understand. Acknowledging this would be a loss of rational control, or at least the illusion of rational control. Though actually, acknowledgment of the power of the unconscious constitutes a gain in awareness. Like gravity, whether we subscribe to the theory or not, it exerts pressure on us all the time.

Relying on an understanding of the unconscious is one of a number of tools we need if we are to succeed in tracking the communication process between partners. Understanding what it takes to create emotional safety involves a consideration of the elements within the second dimension—the emotional subtext we convey by tone of voice or the way we position a remark in the dialogue to indicate, for example, respect or lack of respect for our partners. The elements in second dimension include conscious and unconscious issues.

When tracking the effect of a remark or interaction to devise the best way to support or create emotional safety, we consider the history of emerging consciousness (awareness) of the issue at hand. By way of illustration, think about this situation: Evelyn complains that Terrance does not do his fair share of the housework. He has responded to her by doing more chores around the house. To his surprise, Evelyn states he is taking advantage of her good nature and that she isn't going to stand for it anymore. She speaks to him as if he had ignored her request for him to step up his involvement with the housework.

In response, he takes a deep breath and, as calmly as he can, describes how he has responded to her previous complaints. As he speaks, Evelyn breaks down in tears. When she composes herself, she apologizes to him for complaining about his not doing his share. She tells him that the situation at work has become unbearable. "I have invested all this time and energy but feel so unappreciated there. I feel like no one gives me credit for the work I do, and instead of feeling like I'm part of a team, I feel like an outsider. I get the assignments that no one else wants, and it's really getting to me. I think I was taking it out on you, and that's not fair."

Evelyn had displaced her upset about the job onto Terrance, and then she apologizes for it. Terrance tracks this interaction and takes note of how Evelyn works with herself to be fair to him and, in the end, feels that she treated him fairly. He allows that when she renewed her complaints about his doing his share of the housework, she was in the sway of a strong feeling and that taking out feelings of resentment she had on her job were being dumped on him. In his thinking about it, it makes a difference to him that she was unaware—unconscious—of this displacement process. As soon as she did become aware of it, she owned up to it and apologized to him. Terrance's confidence in Evelyn, his belief that she would not feel comfortable treating him unfairly if she were aware of doing so, and that she would apologize if she felt she had treated him unfairly were all confirmed. This resolution reflects a spirit of compassion within the relationship. Also, because Terrance did not become inflamed when he felt he was being wrongly accused, it afforded Evelyn a chance to sort out her feelings. And after sorting them out, she could share them with him. If the communication process did not feel safe, neither of the partners could have "been there" for each other and worked this through.

The second principle feels true on some level to most people. However, the degree to which it is true is profoundly underestimated. This is the principle: we see what we are looking for. Only that. We formulate expectations about what we anticipate we will see. We then *frequently* fail to notice competing events or trends, even when they are central, large, and well within our purview *if* those events fall outside the range of our expectations. And this is so even if noticing those other events would be important and advantageous for us. In effect, the way we notice things is a process, not an event. And prior to the point at which we interface with whatever we are looking at, we develop a mind-set composed of expectations. Those expectations constrict the parameters of our attention. Our mind-set skews our field of attention to make it more likely we will notice what we expect to see and less likely to notice what we are not expecting to encounter. In countless instances, we do not see elements within our range of vision that we do not expect to be there. "See" in this sense means more than just looking; it means recognizing something for what it is.

Let me illustrate: Within twenty-four hours of the *Challenger* space shuttle explosion, Ulric Nasser, sometimes called the "father of cognitive psychology," conducted a now famous experiment. He had 106 of his undergraduate students at Emory University write out by hand personal accounts of the events surrounding the *Challenger* tragedy. Again, that's within twenty-four hours of the accident. Two and a half years after the event, he contacted these students and had them once again write about their experiences on that day. The second time around, fewer than 10 percent of the subjects wrote accounts that agreed in full with what they had written the first time. One out of four wrote accounts that clashed markedly with their original accounts. Slightly over half of the students agreed with their first account in the main, but the second time around recorded details that conflicted with their first recollections. These discrepancies are not that surprising given the passage of time. The most significant item in this experiment—groundbreaking, in fact—is that when the students were informed of the discrepancies between their current accounts and the accounts that they had jotted down within one day of the accident, they insisted unequivocally that the revised memories were the correct ones. They disavowed the accounts they had written within twenty-four hours of the event, even after being shown that those original reports were logged, signed, and dated in their own handwriting!

This experiment has been replicated in the wake of 9/11, immediately after the assassination attempt on Ronald Reagan, and after other notable and highly visible public events. In all, the results were consistent. Once people committed to a *revised* memory, they discredited their original accounts.

The findings substantiated the notion that human memory goes through revisions. And that as people's accounts of what they recall change, there is a strong tendency toward giving full credence to the new recollection, not the original.

This study has been influential in demonstrating that first-person accounts, including eye-witness testimony, are far less reliable than once believed. And here is the point most relevant for us: people routinely disregard pertinent facts, like authenticated accounts of a day's events that clash with their current mind-sets. Having a fixed mind-set causes them to ignore irrefutable evidence, even when it is presented in a straightforward manner.

Let's take this line of reasoning into the realm of relationships. Gina was in the habit of snooping on her boyfriend, Tim. Primarily, she was looking to see whether he had been conducting a relationship with his ex, Sarah. Gina took every opportunity to access his cell phone. When he napped or showered, she nosed her way into his data.

One particular evening, she believed she had "caught" him. She made a beeline for the room in which he sat, potato chip bag nestled on his lap, watching college basketball on television. Cell phone in hand, she lambasted him with insults and accusations. He countered, "The e-mail that you found, what does it say?"

Running directly to Tim, Gina was so out of sorts she had neglected to read what she assumed would be a red-hot email from Sarah. She stood before him then and read. Her face, which had turned red with anger, now was red with embarrassment. There was nothing flirtatious in the e-mail, nor was there anything contradictory to Tim's long-standing claim that he and Sarah were platonic friends. Silence followed. Had that moment been scored in Hollywood, it would have sounded like a thicket of violins buzzing at dissonant intervals.

Tim stayed calm. "She's in no way a threat to you or to me and you. You know Sarah and I met in college. We lived together for two years, and, as I've told you, the relationship fizzled. We had already stopped being lovers about a year before we stopped living together. She is somebody I know well who knows me well. Before we were a couple, we were friends. We're no longer a couple and we've resumed being friends." Tim looked up and caught Gina's half-smile of defeat. "We speak a few times a year. She thinks you are good for me. I am rooting for her to have a good relationship in her life too. You have nothing to be jealous about.

"What were you doing looking in my cell phone?"

Gina had no defense. They had an understanding that their cell phones were private.

She hung her head. "I'm sorry. I shouldn't have been looking in your cell phone. I won't do it again."

"Please don't tell me you are going to respect my privacy and then continue to do what you are doing. If you do that it's really going to bother me. You know I'm going to find out. And it's not going to be good for us," Tim said.

"I am not going to do it anymore. I hear you. I know I was wrong." Gina said.

"Okay. Do you want to watch the game with me?" He patted the cushion next to him.

Gina later told me, "I saw her name in his inbox and jumped to conclusions. For all my checking on him, I never found anything to justify my suspicions." However, she continued checking on him, and eventually he became aware of this. And he was furious about it.

What was going on, and what did it have to do with mind-set?

Gina was convinced that men lie and cheat, and that Tim in particular did too. There was no evidence of it and, at least on the surface, much to reassure her that this was not what he was doing. All of her snooping could not bring assurance that Tim was trustworthy because the parameters of her investigatory search did not direct her to capture any such information. If Tim's telling of his relationship history was to be taken at face value, nothing pointed to his having been unfaithful when in a committed relationship. Based on her reckoning, Gina acknowledged the absence of any evidence that Tim sought any romantic or sexual relationship outside their own. Yet Gina's snooping continued.

Gina had experiences in her history that made it difficult for her to trust Tim. She had been in more than one close relationship in which she felt blindsided by her partner's infidelity. Her parents had separated as a result of her father's repeated infidelities. She felt safer trying to protect herself from what she thought was going to be the inevitable—finding out there was someone else—than taking her chances on trusting Tim. Her fears of abandonment and betrayal were activated without Tim having done anything provocative, and they preoccupied her.

The first step in the direction of trying to create emotional safety—activating the third dimension of communication—is dependent on the ability to entertain at the least the *possibility* that such a thing can be achieved. I directed a lot of my work with Gina at bringing her to that point.

Is Gina an outlier? Maybe in some respects, owing to the tenacity and single-mindedness of her negative expectations, but she had developed the common pattern of expecting and preparing for the worst and as a result not energizing the creation of emotional safety, not investing energy in validating whatever promotes hope and trust. It's a place many of us start from and from which we can launch into something that feels better. But that takes resolve and persistence.

Based on our personal histories, we form expectations that events similar to those we have already experienced are likely to reoccur. And to the extent that we invest in these expectations, we are less inclined to notice what is novel or what may represent a departure from the past. When we are caught up in dysfunctional communication, negative expectations become a powerful deterrent to envisioning breakthroughs. This is a pervasive trend and largely goes on outside our awareness. If this dynamic is too powerful, we are rendered unable to see anything that would contradict those preconceptions.

To illustrate this second pitfall, I'd like to summarize the *Invisible Gorilla Experiment,* known as the most famous psychological experiment of the past thirty years.

The researchers staged and videotaped a narrative. In it, two groups of college students, one wearing white shirts and the other wearing black, form a circle, and the students in the white shirts pass a basketball only to the other students in white shirts. At the same time, the students in black shirts pass a second basketball only to others in black shirts. The subjects of the experiment, the ones who view the video of the narrative, are instructed to count the number of passes completed by the students in white and to ignore those completed by students in black. One final instruction before subjects view the tape is given: Both passes completed on a bounce and those completed without touching the ground must be included in the final tally of passes as long as they begin with a player in a white shirt and are caught by another player in a white shirt.

Then the subjects are shown the tape, which is less than a minute long. After the tape is viewed, subjects are asked to jot down the total number of passes completed by the white-shirted players. The tally is generally very accurate, indicating that subjects understood the directions and carried them out.

Although it is never mentioned beforehand, in the middle of the experiment, a female student dressed head to toe in a gorilla costume parades into the middle of the circle, around which the others are tossing their basketballs, and remains at the center of the scene for a full eight seconds. During this time she pounds her chest with her fists and then exits.

After the experimenters collect the response cards on which the number of completed passes is written, they ask, "By the way, did you notice anything unusual during the experiment?" Fully half of the subjects reply that they hadn't seen anything out of the ordinary in the video. They are then asked specifically if they had seen a gorilla. Fifty percent of the subjects reply, "What gorilla?" They have no recollection of having seen a gorilla walk through the center of the circle in which the students were passing the ball. They were looking for balls passed and caught by the white-uniformed students. They saw what they were looking for. They did not see what they were not expecting to see, even though it's hard to imagine what might have stood out and captured their attention more than a five and a half foot gorilla in the midst of the procedure, pounding its chest for about 15 percent of the total time they viewed the experiment. How could so many report not having witnessed or been aware of the gorilla at all?

What's the lesson? When we study a situation with intent to find *certain* information—that is, when we have a fixed mind-set defined by a task that determines our mission as viewers—we home in on what we are searching for. We find what we expect to find. We have a pronounced tendency to constrict our focus so that anything irrelevant to the reason we have given ourselves for viewing simply does not register. Reverse corollary: if you want to see something, it is enormously advantageous to target it, to maintain conscious intention of noticing that thing—for example, something that might connect to creating emotional safety.

Imagine how different the outcome of the experiment would have been if after being instructed to count bounce passes and passes that do not touch the ground, the subjects were also told to be sure to notice if a gorilla appeared at any time during the experiment. Expectations have a profound effect on perception. It's a simple point not many would argue against. But few take into account how pervasive and powerful its effect is when it comes to determining the course of a relationship.

Gina was looking for what was familiar to her. Her focus was constricted. She was busily focused on collecting evidence that Tim was not trustworthy. Were there a contrary perspective—that he was trustworthy—she would not have noticed evidence for it.

Partners who keep detailed (actual or metaphorical) complaint ledgers of grievances and justifications for why their partners are at fault in their relationship do more than accentuate the negative. They put themselves into a condition in which they are likely to fail to notice new developments either in their partners' behavior or in the circumstances that might give rise to a new and more healthy direction in their communication.

To participate in a change process, it is a great advantage to keep in mind that the desired positive change is possible. The trick is to figure out what that way is and attempt to actualize it. If the new trend gets off to a sputtering start, the tragedy of many relationships is that partners are so locked into the purview created by their power struggle that they fail to see it, validate it, and develop it. If you wish to know the outcome of my work with Gina and Tim, turn to Appendix 3.

The invisible gorilla experiment has been replicated widely, and the results are consistent. Attempts have been made to introduce this logic into criminal court cases in which the issue has to do with proximity of a bystander to a criminal activity. The assumption that a person very close to the scene of a crime must have known what was occurring is being contested. For that matter, the new research on the unreliability of eye-witness testimony—reference the *Challenger* experiment on this—is another live issue that has been challenged in courtrooms all over the nation.

This perspective helps us understand from an additional vantage point how and why the change process is so difficult. What can balance this tendency to see only what we expect to see? Mindful awareness of the here and now operates as a corrective to this inability to see the "invisible gorilla" within our experiences. Although this takes dedication to achieve, what is sometimes called *beginner's mind* is an idea that many find inspiring. In a nutshell, evolved from Buddhist thinking, beginner's mind involves a commitment to seeing things in a fresh manner, without expectations or filters, as if you are witnessing what you are looking at for the first time. If practiced diligently through use of meditation and other mind-clearing practices, it is a way of thinking about approaching information that can reduce the influence of preconceptions and unhelpful expectations.

We want our relationships to flow organically in a positive direction. The problem with this expectation is that many of us equate an organic flow in a relationship with *an effortless flow.*

A relationship's well-being is *not* pillared on its ability to *resist* the wear and tear of time. Instead, the stresses of unavoidable change can be softened by the acceptance and compassion that partners extend to one another. This creates the strength and secure attachment that we all crave. Flexibility, a willingness to extend while guarding against overextending, and maintaining a sense of purpose within the love relationship and within a community that brings meaning and purpose are elements that protect you through good and hard times alike. There are no magical romantic solutions. But that doesn't mean romance is not real or that it cannot survive. It just doesn't have to be magical. It can be on a human scale, which, when brought anywhere close to potential, is awesome.

Creating and nurturing better communication involves coming to an understanding about what you and your partner mean by improvements in communication. After that, following through by making a point of catching your partner doing things that create emotional safety and validating him is an important next step. Look for what is going right. Although dealing with negative trends is inevitable, keeping a focus on developing the positive takes effort, concentration, intention, and attention. Nothing energizes the trend of improved communication more effectively than mutual recognition of efforts and willingness to bring those improvements into the culture of the relationship.

Clearly, Gina was not looking to find Tim doing what was right. She did not consciously practice the creation of emotional safety *for the relationship*. Because I have written a lot in this chapter about Gina's part in this interaction, it may seem as if I am blaming her for the difficulties in communication. This is not so. Although I am not going to go into them here, Tim has his own issues as well. Even though he was not having an outside relationship, he had ways in which he failed to reassure Gina when it might have made a difference. Except in the rarest of circumstances—or in instances of abuse of any kind—problems between partners cannot be attributed to either partner alone. They certainly cannot be solved that way.

Gina's preoccupation with not reliving her past and not reexperiencing being surprised by a betrayal left her unable to clarify ways in which she could differentiate the present from the past. She was focused on seeing whether older patterns were joined with the present. In her anticipation, she relived the coming of what had already occurred. This is why an intentional focus on understanding the here and now, in terms of its possibilities for containing new elements, can be so liberating for partners caught in the grip of fears.

There is a great deal of sadness in a story like Gina and Tim's because, despite their difficulties, they did care about each other and were able to share some memorable good times. Looking at it from Gina's perspective, in a sense they were faced with a double whammy of the two pitfalls we discussed in this chapter. She was not aware of much of what motivated her to destroy the trust in the relationship. She was aware of the anger associated with having been betrayed in former relationships, but during the time that she was with Tim she remained unable to face the sadness and fear that lay beneath that anger. Her commitment to not seeing herself in this way left her unable to build emotional safety. Also, as I've already touched on, she was unable to draw any reassurance from her continued failure to discover anything but evidence substantiating innocence of infidelity on Tim's part—the "invisible gorilla" in their story—which might have soothed her worries if only she had been able to listen with a trusting heart to what he was saying to her.

Part Three

Using Neuroscientific Breakthroughs for Better Relationships

CHAPTER ELEVEN

Limbic Learnings

*Love and compassion are necessities,
not luxuries. Without them humanity
cannot survive.*

—Dalai Lama

I have to admit that when I began learning about neuroscience, I found it somewhat intimidating. The names of the parts of the brain alone were long and Latin and confusing. As I began feeling more comfortable with the material, I found that many powerful neuroscientific concepts are straightforward and highly accessible. By grasping them, we gain insight into the way our minds and emotions function in real-time.

Part of doing judicious and effective work in healing any relationship involves discriminating between what can be changed and what must be accepted. The neural setup, the way in which we process emotions, is something we cannot change; we need to accept and understand it. In this brief chapter I will outline what I believe are the essentials.

Our brains are essentially pattern decoders. The amygdala, located in the center of the brain, is part of the limbic system and is sometimes called "the brain within the brain," or "the emotional core of the brain." It receives inputs from all senses as well as visceral inputs. Its purpose is to determine on the basis of messages it receives whether or not the here and now situation is safe.

If and when the amygdala detects danger, it sounds a hormonal alarm famously known as the fight-or-flight response. This response includes elevated heartbeat, activation of the sweat glands in the hands and feet, increased blood flow to the brain and large muscle groups, and dilated pupils. These are the systems that get activated.

Here's what gets deactivated during the fight-or-flight response: the cerebral cortex. That is the part of the brain that has evolved most recently. It enables us to reflect, to evaluate how we feel and think about what we are feeling and thinking, and to fan out our options and consider them before taking action.

It's as if a toggle switch in the brain can be set at only one of two positions at a time. Either the limbic system is on and simultaneously the cerebral cortex is shut down; or the limbic system is off and the cerebral cortex is active.

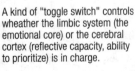

A kind of "toggle switch" controls wheather the limbic system (the emotional core) or the cerebral cortex (reflective capacity, ability to prioritize) is in charge.

When the cerebral cortex is online, the body is primed to enact an instinctual response quite different from fight-or-flight. It is known as the *relaxation response*, and although much less well-known than the fight-or-flight response, it is dynamic and essential to our well-being. It is characterized by lowered heartbeat, enhanced social engagement capacity, and, of course, enhanced cortical functionality.

Conversations about difficulties in relationship go poorly and are routinely destructive if conducted while the limbic system is activated. Anger and fear impair our judgment because when we are angry, the part of the brain that we use to make judgments is not available to us!

Nonetheless, when angered, we often feel energized and seek to unload our anger on the object of our wrath; often, whoever is close at hand gets the fallout.

Lenny and Tristan, a couple I worked with, routinely found themselves in destructive shouting matches. When I explained the basic principles that guide activation of the limbic system and the toggle switch concept, they listened carefully. Lenny, more than Tristan, was prone to flying into hot rages with minimal provocation. Tristan's inability to tolerate Lenny's fits of anger had been their presenting problem.

As we progressed in our work together, I asked Lenny, "When you pursue conversation with Tristan while angry, do you ever have good results?"

"Not really," he said.

"The thing is, Lenny, as you can tell from what I was saying about the limbic system, when you go after Tristan in anger, you are effectively functioning with half a brain, and, in terms of reasoned problem solving, it's not the most useful half. The part of you that can figure out what is in your best interest and help you to keep track of your priorities is off-line. Do you want to risk your relationship on behaviors chosen when your decision-making ability is not available to you?"

Putting this kind of information out to someone bluntly like this sometimes backfires. However, Lenny had told me explicitly that he very much wanted to have better control of his anger. Having his anger described this way gave him pause. He said that it had been a factor in what became a series of cognitive and behavioral changes as a result of his gaining better control of how and when he expressed his anger.

By way of an illustration, the following is a snippet of conversation between a different set of partners who came to me for help in disentangling themselves from a chronic and destructive pattern of mutual limbic arousal. They were talking about their plans for the upcoming summer.

"I want to hear your ideas on the subject," Talia said.

"Okay, I'm ready to tell you what I think. Can you just hold off and not say anything for a few minutes while I get my thoughts out?" Kim said.

"I said I want to hear what you have to say. Can you tell me?" Talia sounded a little peeved.

"I will. Only don't interrupt me. Would you please be quiet while I'm talking?" Kim's amygdala was firing.

"All right already. Talk. I'm listening. I told you three times that I am listening. You've got the floor." Talia heated up more.

Kim raised her voice dramatically. "I'm going to tell you what I'm thinking if you'd just stop talking."

Talia spoke even louder. "I am sick and tired of you telling me to be quiet." She stood and stomped out of the room.

Those of us who have lived with such ill-fated attempts at communication can appreciate how demoralizing they can feel. Think about how little it takes to generate angry/defensive responses once this mind-set is triggered, typical of chronic limbic activation.

Kim and Talia both function at a deficit. They have little or no opportunity to consider possibilities for creating emotional safety because of mutual limbic arousal. Although it is temporary, they are, in these moments, biologically, not just psychologically, impaired. This is why acquiring techniques to calm a chronically activated limbic system is essential to creating emotional safety, or what the mindfulness movement often refers to as "inner peace."

Creating peace in your relationship and creating peace within yourself are parallel processes that must both be developed as a three-dimensional perspective is acquired.

Here is another analogy for this either/or balance of capacities that I find useful. Imagine the limbic system being located at one end of a seesaw. The frontal cortex sits at the other end of the seesaw.

When the side representing the limbic system comes down to the ground, it is in the activated position. When this happens, the other side, the one that represents frontal cortex functionality, floats in a state of disconnection. As long as the limbic system remains in the down (or "on") position, the frontal cortex makes a negligible contribution to psychic functioning.

The more time the limbic system operates in the on setting, the more likely it is to continue to do so. Why? Because a chronically activated person filters experience through a lens that highlights (is on the lookout for) the possibility that danger lurks; the limbic system develops a bias toward interpreting the possibility of danger as potentially imminent in more and more situations.

A sight or sound may not signal danger in itself but may be associated with something that does. Then this secondary association may be linked to another association until any event that invites attention brings up the possibility of being a threat. This pattern is known as hypervigilance and is common among individuals who have experienced trauma.

In certain instances, quiet or a lack of stimulation may provoke a limbic response as the individual may associate silence or the lack of stimulus with prior danger that was preceded with a lull. It is easy to see that nearly anything that is perceived can become a cause for alarm, a cause for the deactivation of the cortical capacities. In a case like this, the frontal cortex, with all its capacities, stays disconnected, irrelevant, and inactive, unable to make a positive contribution to the mind-brain in which it exists.

So what tools are on hand to reconfigure this imbalance and get the frontal cortex back online? I have mentioned some of the methods that are commonly used: meditation, appropriate exercise, recreation, and so on. Another source of calm is greater understanding of the mechanisms that can create emotional safety, such as holding the *intention* to think before reacting to a given situation.

Awareness of the requirements for creating emotional safety helps change the odds in favor of being able to create it. The descriptions in this book are meant to help you conceptualize how our neurological system is set up. This can move you in the direction of being able to strengthen your ability to send intentional signals to direct yourself toward experiencing emotional safety and optimism. Learning that your neuro-physiological system (see Chapter Twelve, the discussion of the polyvagal system) possesses the ability to expand its functionality toward a heightened experience of emotional safety can help validate your potential to achieve this state of mind. Understanding the advantages of a learning mind-set moves us in a hopeful direction. This can counter chronic limbic arousal and the impulsive-, fear-, or anger-driven responses that come with it.

Conscious attempts to reflect on what is going on at the moment that the feeling of being overwhelmed is sensed can bring the frontal cortex online, at least momentarily. Here's a simple trauma first-aid technique that illustrates this point: If you should feel you are becoming flooded with any emotion (fear, anxiety, anger, etc.), pretend for a moment that you have a straw in your mouth. Then form your lips into a tight circle and release your breath in a slow steady stream of air. The act of attempting this simple task brings your intentionality online. It slows down the limbic response and can calm you, depending on how strong the original feeling is. Try it the next time you feel uneasy.

Also, simply having a contingency plan, something you can do, in the event that you feel shaken can reduce feelings of helplessness that often accompany limbic arousal.

EXERCISE 11.1

LIMBIC LIMBO QUIZ

Many have an aversion to tests. Rather than help them to remember what they've been studying, "test anxiety" causes them to forget everything they have tried to learn and taints the information going forward. Presumably this has to do with the fear of being judged. On the other hand, new research on education holds that when presented with new material, students learn from the experience if they are held accountable for knowing what they have learned. This is the rationale for understanding that surgeons have a continuously steep learning curve throughout their careers—they never stop learning and integrating new material—because if they do not get the desired results, they are immediately made aware of that fact by the patient's condition. In effect, each procedure is a test, and the results are immediately evident. Other kinds of physicians who do not have direct access to the results of their interventions tend to hit a plateau, where they report they are no longer developing. They become stuck without the feedback that would result if their judgments were tested by concrete results delivered in conjunction with the service they render.

To help you to integrate the new material on the limbic system and cerebral cortex, I want to give you something on which you can test your knowledge without invoking the forget-inducing test anxiety. This is my solution. The questions below are true-false. You can challenge yourself with them. Unless a question begins with the phrase *Is this true?* it is a true statement. Items that begin with that phrase *Is this true?* are not true. Some of the items introduce terms that are straightforward but haven't been used in the chapter. The idea is to introduce you to a few more important and useful ideas. So you have the key, you are poised to integrate the material with minimal, if any anxiety. Why present material this way? Because learning in a game context is generally more fun.

True or False?

1) Is this true? A person is best able to listen carefully to her partner when her limbic system is activated.

2) A person is unable to listen carefully to his partner when his limbic system is activated.

3) When the limbic system is activated, a person is responding to a threat to her emotional or physical safety. By the way, emotional and physical pain are processed in the very same center in the brain.

4) Is this true? When danger of any kind is sensed, the limbic system goes quiet.

5) The fight-or-flight (or freeze) response is evidence that the limbic system has been activated. The word *triggered* is often used as a synonym for *activated*.

6) When the fight-or-flight instinct is not active, a relaxation response, also a basic instinct, becomes activated.

7) The relaxation response is less well-known than the fight-or-flight response but has been researched extensively and confirmed as a genuine instinctive response.

8) When we are up-regulated, it means that our nervous systems are "revved" up. This means that the limbic system is aroused. It means that a system within the brain has provoked the limbic system to sound an alarm and mobilize the body's fight-or-flight response.

9) Is this true? Under severe threat to life humans do *not* exhibit a "freeze" response. That is common to and limited to a reptilian response pattern.

10) When our systems are down-regulated, it means that our nervous systems have confirmed, whether this is so or not, that the situation both within our bodies and in our immediate environments feels safe and nonthreatening. Down-regulated is associated with relaxation and safety.

11) For the most part, when we down-regulate our nervous systems, it means that defensive energies are halted and social engagement capacities are boosted. Under these conditions we are at our best in terms of having intimate conversations and responding empathically.

12) When down-regulated, we are able to make the best use of the decision-making centers of our brains. When the body is calm, we are able to think most clearly about the thoughts and feelings we are experiencing and the thoughts and feelings that our partners communicate to us.

13) Is this true? When the cerebral cortex is fully functional, the limbic system is sometimes aroused.

14) Is this true? When up-regulated, we are at our best in terms of empathizing with our partners.

15) When down-regulated, we can appreciate the difficulties of staying in emotional contact and articulate concern and compassion toward ourselves and our partners.

16) When we are down-regulated, we are at our best in terms of tuning in to our partners emotions accurately.

17) When the limbic system is not aroused, the cerebral cortex goes online.

18) The cerebral cortex houses our decision-making and reflective capacities.

19) Is this true? The limbic system is *not* referred to as the emotional core of the brain or ever as "the emotional brain within the brain."

20) Is this true? Our best decisions result from not paying attention to our emotions. Good decision making is not a blend of emotion and reason but a function of good reasoning ability.

CHAPTER TWELVE

HARD Science

What is adaptive to survival is not
intelligence and it's not aggression.
It's the ability to cope with change.

—Leon Megginson (paraphrasing Charles Darwin)

I n recent years, two bodies of important research have caused
leaders in the psychology field to rethink and reconfigure their
understanding of emotion, communication, attachment, and self-
regulation. My goal here is to explain and simplify, without over-
simplifying, the nature of these contributions. They have powerful
implications that are applicable to learning what it takes to make
couples' relationships better. Understanding Stephen Porges's and Jaak
Panksepp's contributions will help us to see how the idea of three-
dimensional communication rests on hard scientific evidence.

Stephen Porges's pioneering work in neuroscience has been credited with bringing about a fundamental shift in the way scientists
understand emotion. Through his research we understand *emotional safety* from a neurobiological perspective, as a measurable and

quantifiable phenomenon. As you read through this book, you see that term, *emotional safety*, again and again. You may be assuming that I am speaking about it from a philosophical or psychological standpoint. Not really. I am primarily concerned with it from a biological standpoint, and that perspective would be mere conjecture without Dr. Porges's contributions.

In the previous chapter, I reviewed some basic information concerning the dynamics of the limbic system and explained through use of the toggle switch and seesaw metaphors that only one or the other, that is, *either* the limbic system *or* the cerebral cortex, can achieve full functionality at the same time.

Porges's work introduces us to different set of three neurological subsystems that are tethered together and organized into what he calls the "polyvagal system." (See Figure 12.1.) When any one of the three subsystems is lit, the other two are dark. What determines which of the three polyvagal subsystems becomes active at any given time? It is the degree of safety that is sensed in the internal and external environment by specialized parts of the nervous system itself. By grasping the logic of how and why this occurs, we achieve a substantial insight into how our nervous systems process emotion.

What is the purpose of knowing about this? In order to summon our greatest potential for connection, it helps to know what equipment is available for us to work with. By the way, that equipment is who we are, our highest potential not expressed in terms of hopes or dreams concerning what we might achieve but in embodied capacities that are *already* developed within us. To point ourselves toward activating our most sophisticated evolutionary functionality, awareness of what we have to work with is not just educational but inspiring.

What are the three subsystems that make up the polyvagal system? The most advanced, the one we are most interested in, Porges has dubbed the "social engagement system." Through reception of a

3-TIER POLYVAGAL SYSTEM

Tier #1
Social Engagement System
When activated? When safety is detected; absence of any threat.
Most highly evolved subsystem
Neo-mammalian
Corresponds to Human Brain

Tier #2
Resonates with Fight-or-Flight Response
When Activated? When danger is detected.
Midrange subsystem (in terms of evolution)
Mammalian
Corresponds to Tiger Brain

Tier #3
Resonates with Freeze Response
Activated when life and death threat is detected
Most primitive subsystem
Reptilian
Corresponds to Snake Brain

Figure 12.1 3-Tier Polyvagal System

sequence of hormone-driven messages, this system is up and running only when the polyvagal nervous system registers that we are safe. This safety is both physical and emotional, internal and external. When safety is confirmed, the social engagement system activates. The process by which the nervous system determines the degree of safety that exists within and surrounding us at any given time is called *neuroception*, a term Porges coined when he discovered the process.

If a lack of safety is detected, the social engagement system goes dark immediately. Then a secondary system lights up. This secondary system, allied to the fight-or-flight response, sometimes called the mobilization system, remains active for as long as the threat to safety remains.

If the threat escalates, the most primitive subsystem (immobilization) is activated. This subsystem parallels what is sometimes referred to as the freeze response. It activates only when an imminent life-or-death threat is detected.

Should the threat disappear completely, the social engagement system lights up again and stays on for as long as conditions are deemed safe.

When threat is detected, blood flows to the large muscle groups in the body so as to facilitate capability for fight or flight. With no threat, an abundant supply of blood flows to the smaller muscle groups, including the facial musculature and central auditory pathways. With the added blood supply, the forty-two facial muscles take on superb sensitivity. Significant changes also occur in the inner ear. Once energized, the social engagement system is primed to utilize advanced evolutionary features to connect with others.

Let's track how this occurs when two individuals meet. Taking it from the vantage point of one, whom we will call the viewer and the other who is being viewed, let's trace the initial social engagement that leads to an empathic connection.

First, the viewer takes special notice of the other's face, a prime source of information about whether or not the other represents a threat. If the viewer feels safe and determines that the other does not constitute a threat, a complex neurobiological process begins: empathy.

From a neurobiological perspective, what do we mean by an empathic process? Once the viewer sees the other's face, he automatically and unconsciously creates an instantaneous kinetic impression of it upon his own face. In other words, within a flicker of time, the viewer mimics the expression of the other. The viewer, in effect, encodes the image of the other using his facial musculature as a kind of notepad upon which to record the image, which is sent to the appropriate brain center to be decoded.

The viewer transfers information he has gathered first visually and then kinesthetically to a cortical center where specialized cells, referred to as mirror neurons, facilitate a cross-referencing process. The way specific muscles are tensed or released corresponds to variations and gradations in emotion. The viewer's brain compares and contrasts the mimicked expression with trace memories that identify how the viewer has felt when he displayed a similar facial expression. This process informs the viewer as to what he would be feeling *if his own face had originated the expression* that the person being viewed wears on his face.

This is the reason we think of empathy as an "inside-out" process. Through it we go beyond identifying the emotion we see in the other to actually feeling from within what it signifies.

The neurobiological aspect of the process of empathy does not depend on being able to take a leap of imagination into the other's consciousness. It has to do with utilizing great sensitivity to one's own nervous system; it is an *embodied* process of intimate communication within the self and between the self and the other.

When a person is feeling socially engaged, he is able to access associations to when and how he has experienced his own emotions. For this reason, empathy involves 1) the ability to access what another feels, *and* 2) the ability to access one's *own* range and history of emotional experiences and responses. Being emotionally in sync with another requires that we be emotionally in sync with our own self-experiences. This is not a touchy-feely presumption; it is a neuroscientific fact.

Empathy can also be characterized as an information-processing loop. It is a tool our species possesses that has evolved to track one another's feelings. The prerequisite for utilizing our optimal empathic ability is feeling safe.

An experiment conducted in 2011 by Professor Tanya Chartrand of Duke University and Assistant Professor David Neal of the University of Southern California found that women who had received

Botox facial treatments, which temporarily immobilized their facial muscles, had impaired ability to identify both negative and positive emotion displayed in photographs of human eyes shown to them. The experiment confirmed that subtle mimicry of the facial expression contributes to the ability to identify emotion in others, which these subjects were unable to perform because Botox effectively immobilized the facial muscles surrounding their eyes.

The change in our hearing when the social engagement system is active is fascinating. When we feel safe, a tiny bone within the inner ear shifts. This blocks high and low frequencies, leaving our midrange reception with heightened sensitivity. The midrange frequencies that are enhanced when the social engagement system is in its "turned on" position are precisely those that the human voice produces. Because of this shift, ability to detect nuance and subtle emotional inference from the tone and timbre of a human voice is upgraded.

The second cutting edge neuroscientist I want to briefly discuss is Jaak Panksepp. Like Porges, Panksepp revolutionized the field of affective neuroscience through extensive research in delineating and tracking emotion. Panksepp's contributions have been a significant part of the sea change that has occurred over the past thirty years, and that has placed emotion, rather than cognition, in the forefront of psychological and neuroscientific research.

Panksepp identifies seven separate executive operating systems within the human nervous system. The systems correspond to emotions—RAGE, FEAR, SEEKING, LUST, CARE, PANIC, PLAY—but represent more than simply those emotions. Panksepp capitalizes the subsystems to emphasize that they represent entire neural networks that come into play when these emotions are active.

Each of the seven forms its own command center and when activated utilizes experience in the service of its own mission. Two of the seven subsystems he describes function in coordination with the fight-or-flight response: FEAR and RAGE. You might say that each subsystem represents a subpersonality that when active responds to and considers experience differently from each of the others.

Let's see how this works with Tony and Donald, who attend a party together and end up quarrelling afterward. Donald had become angry at the party because he felt that Tony did not pay enough attention to him when they were there.

Tony felt dejected as a result of being confronted by Donald's fearsome anger, which in the context of the Panksepp material we can think of as corresponding to activation of the RAGE network.

Their dialogue illustrates the idea that when either partner operates out of a specific command center, it is important to keep in mind that there is more to them than that particular network.

Tony: He's furious with me. No matter what I do or say, he finds a way to turn it into something negative.

Donald: It's not hard to find a way to turn what you say into something negative because you say so much that is negative. I don't turn it into anything it isn't.

Therapist: So you find yourself getting angry at Tony frequently?

Donald: Yes, I do.

Therapist [to Tony]: So Donald is validating your perception that he is angry with you frequently. What I'd like to do is explore the quality of Donald's anger. Would that be okay with you?

Tony: [nods]

Donald: Okay.

Therapist: Donald, I understand that you get angry with Tony. We spent a long time last session discussing how you were angry with him at the party. What I wonder is whether anger is the only feeling you have toward Tony, even when you feel anger toward him.

Donald: What do you mean?

Therapist: I mean, you were angry at him at the party because he hadn't stayed with you, and you said that you had looked forward to spending time with him, but when you actually were at the party, you felt as if you had come by yourself.

Donald: That's right.

Therapist: So does that mean you missed his companionship at the party?

Donald: Yes. I did. And that's why I was angry.

Therapist: So you missed Tony, and that was mixed in with the anger. Tony, were you aware of that?

Tony: No.

Therapist: So he was aware of the anger, but not of the other part, the part of you [looking at Donald] that was missing him. I'm wondering how you feel about that, Donald?

Donald: Well, if I didn't care about whether he was there, why would I get angry if we were separated? I thought he understood that I was angry because I wanted his company.

Therapist: Do you think it's possible that once he recognized you were angry, he didn't think much more about anything else you might have felt? Your anger may have obscured those other feelings, particularly feelings of wanting to be close to him? Or your anger might have been intimidating or threatening in some other way, causing him to keep his distance. Does that make sense?

Donald: I guess so.

Therapist: I'd like to discuss this in such a way that you don't feel blamed. [Pause] I'm noticing that Tony picked up on your anger, probably because when that part of you gets activated, a lot of energy comes into focus around that feeling. And that's all he was able to recognize. Is it important to you, Donald, that other sides, other parts of your personality other than anger, come across to Tony? Do you want him to have a sense that they are there?

Donald: Of course I want him to have a deeper sense of what I feel.

Therapist: Tony, do you see that even when Donald is angry, at least in some situations, probably many situations, there are other parts of him that come into play as well? That may not be visible in the moment.

Tony: I hear it, but I'm not sure if I believe it.

Therapist: Would you believe it if you heard Donald talk about these things in the moment when you are having these exchanges?

Tony: Probably.

Therapist: Donald, how do you feel about Tony having the belief, up until this point, that most of the time you are angry at him there is nothing more than rage at play? What does that say to you?

Donald: It says I guess I'm not doing as good a job as I could of conveying my feelings. That's not the kind of outcome I want for our conversations.

In this dialogue, Tony finds it comforting and somewhat surprising to learn that even when Donald is angry, he is aware of wanting to stay connected to Tony. Donald's willingness to hold himself accountable for doing a better job of communicating his feelings to Tony also helps Tony feel safer in discussing Donald's anger with him.

When partners express anger, particularly extreme anger, it is common for the object of their anger, often their partners, to become alienated and assume that their partners have nothing but anger to share with them. Taking a page from attachment theory, where anger is in a relationship, more often than not there is frustration about an insufficiently secure attachment. The issue often has more to do with wanting to be connected than anger, per se. Yet when the RAGE network is turned on, it is hard to calm it. It is part of our instinctual fight-or-flight response. It is important for partners to know that for communication to occur after anger subsides, it is necessary to activate one of the other command centers dedicated to feeling connected in various ways. CARING and LUST obviously fit in, in different ways, with possibilities for closeness. SEEKING and PLAY are modalities that lend themselves to finding new solutions to old problems. The PANIC system has to do with fear produced by feelings of abandonment and therefore also lends itself to possibilities for reconnection. The idea is that as partners explore how they are relating in terms of creating emotional safety, it helps to have a sense, using the Panksepp schema, of which response mode is active. Certain approaches will work when PLAY is activated that would fail disastrously if FEAR or RAGE were in command.

When couples come in for therapy, they sometimes ask for specific steps and techniques they can follow to feel secure they are reconnecting. However, in approaching any attempt at relational healing, it is important to be aware that success or failure is often dictated not by the technique being used but by the mind-set, including the emotional operating system (whichever one of the seven) the partner is functioning within at the time that the work is being attempted.

PANKSEPP'S 7 PRIMAL EMOTIONS:

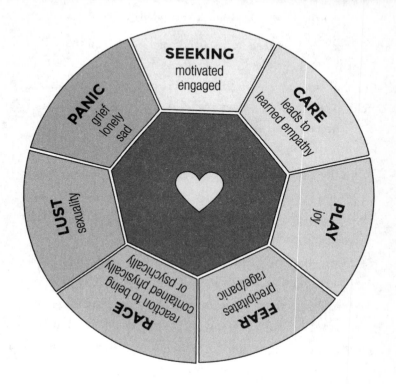

Each is a neural subsystem that dominates emotional functionality when activated. For example if the PANIC system is activated during a surgical procedure crying behavior is elicited. In order to conduct effective couples therapy, partners must not simply be focused on the dialogue at hand, but must be focused from within one of the neural command centers that will enable them to listen empathetically and respond on that wavelength.

When partners are functioning within the RAGE, FEAR, or PANIC modalities, the work at hand is to deactivate the perspective and shift gears by moving into one of the other centers that allows for, rather than defends against, interpersonal contact.

What allows for the internal flexibility to make such changes? Emotional safety.

EXERCISE 12.1

Empathy Awareness

Read each of the fifteen items listed below, and on a sheet of paper write down whether the statement reflects the way you act/feel in your relationship with your partner. If you are not in a relationship at the moment, how you would have responded in your most recent relationship? After completing the exercise, feel free to turn to Appendix 2 and compare and contrast your comments with mine.

1) In the past two weeks I can recall at least one situation in which I gave my partner the benefit of a doubt.

2) I make a special effort to have my partner understand the ways in which I believe we see things eye to eye.

3) Even when my partner and I disagree, I rarely feel like I can't understand why he feels the way he does.

4) I would say that I am as interested in understanding my partner as I am in having my partner understand me.

5) When my partner and I disagree, I am curious to understand how and why she feels as she does.

6) I criticize my partner too frequently.

7) When I criticize my partner, he usually takes it the wrong way.

8) I do not believe I do this, but my partner complains that I talk down to him.

9) I don't mean to do it, but there are times I find myself talking down to my partner.

10) When I argue with my partner, most of the time I find myself waiting for him to finish talking so I can make my point.

11) Patience is something I've developed and learned to help me create understandings.

12) I want my partner to understand me. That is to say, I'd like her to be familiar not only with what my opinions are but with how I've come to the opinions that I have.

13) When my partner tells me how he feels about something, I do not ask how he came to feel that way. I feel that understanding him on that level is almost an invasion of his privacy.

14) I recall when I first understood that my partner's political leanings differed from my own in significant ways. I wondered whether this would create an insurmountable problem for us.

15) My partner has a very different relationship with his family of origin than I do. I recognize that I can't change his relationship with his parents, but often wish that I could.

Conversational Interlude 3

Dysfunctional Communication Is So Exhausting
Where's the empathy?

Olivia: Do you understand what I'm telling you?

Norton: Yes.

Olivia: That's good. Tell me—I'm not so sure myself.

Norton: Then why are you telling me if you're not sure what you want to say yourself?

Olivia: Because I want to find out what I want, and this is the closest I can come to it.

Norton: Really?

Olivia: Really.

Norton: Okay. I heard you say that you want me to listen more carefully to what you are saying so that I really understand what you're trying to say.

Olivia: That's it. Can you do that?

Norton: Of course. Don't you think I already do that?

Olivia: I can't tell. But if you have to ask me about it, I have my doubts.

Norton: Well, you're entitled to your doubts. There's nothing wrong with that.

Olivia: Oh, really?

Norton: Really.

Olivia: Well, that's not what I started out wanting to talk about, but that's interesting.

Norton: I'm glad you find it interesting. I find it infuriating.

Olivia: Really?

Norton: Yes, really. There are doubts strewn all over the place, and who needs them?

Olivia: I thought you said that I was entitled to mine and that there was nothing wrong with them.

Norton: Yes, I said that. But that doesn't mean I like it. There are some things you just have to accept.

Olivia: Oh, so no wonder I have my doubts.

Norton: Right. No wonder.

CHAPTER THIRTEEN

Conclusion

By defining our goal more clearly—
by making it seem more manageable
and less remote—we can help all people
to see it, to draw hope from it, and
to move irresistibly toward it.

—John F. Kennedy

I participated in a talk show on the Sex Talk Radio network. The subject of the program was boundaries in relationship. Two others were participating in the conversation. The moderator and her sidekick emphasized keeping boundaries strong, staying in control. Situations definitely exist in relationships in which strong boundaries are needed for self-protection.

What Is Between Boundaries?

Firm boundaries make sense when staying protected is the prime objective. When couples in long-term relationships find themselves mutually committed to these kinds of standoffs, however, healing can't

261

happen. It is not the posture, the firm boundaries, that is problematic. But if they are held inflexibly, the relationship is paralyzed.

So how can boundaries be as protective as needed but also flexible? The *intention* to keep them responsive makes the difference. An active, conscious commitment to working toward greater openness is needed. But that can't really happen unless emotional safety prevails. If it doesn't, shifting into a more open and less defensive stance makes no sense.

Our mind-sets, the way we enter into interactions, determine a great deal about what we end up accomplishing or leaving undone in terms of relationship healing. Boundaries can be problematic, but it is the space between the boundaries in which the real work has to get done. The garden exists outside the walls. Each partner has to take responsibility for the atmosphere between herself and her partner. That space has to be monitored with care, determination, and vision. If it is a wasteland depleted of warmth and lacking signs that sincere invitations to make contact are welcomed, the path to improving communication is blocked. The immediate problem becomes getting it unblocked.

"Weak" boundaries aren't necessarily the opposite of strong boundaries. If strong boundaries are healthy, the result of mindful intentionality and not compulsive defensiveness, the true opposite would be flexible boundaries. They can be firm when that is needed but relaxed and open when you wish them to be. The key is not the relative strength of the boundaries but your sense of control over them. Your intentionality must remain strong so that you can act in your own best interest in the moment. What you want is freedom from impingement, exploitation, or cruelty, as well as freedom to connect when and if you wish to.

The power struggle in many relationships becomes the medium through which all emotion is exchanged. In these situations, the enemy of love is the power struggle itself and the way it hypnotizes partners into focusing on not getting hurt. Then not getting hurt morphs into not exposing vulnerability, and that devolves further into feeling alone within the relationship. Daring to engage emotionally becomes a thing of the past. Can this pattern be broken? It can with courage and a reliable strategy.

Three-dimensional communication offers a gentle challenge to this focus on the power struggle. It offers a way to downplay the debate on who is right and who is wrong, whose boundaries are weak and whose are strong, and replaces the power struggle with the challenge of creating emotional safety.

Too often when couples experience frustration because they are unable to communicate effectively, their frustration gets redirected against their partners. And that sets the stage for a counterattack. This problem of the inability to communicate soon recedes into the background. Opportunities to work together to make things better become increasingly distant. Disappointment and disillusionment poison conversation further. Eventually partners live in an atmosphere of constant deprivation. The road back from the disconnection—the solution to this syndrome—is paved with validation. And appreciation. And acknowledgment. Compassionate realization of each other's suffering registers and sets a new tone. Someone asked me, "What key is that new tone in?" The new tonality is "If we do nothing we can hang on to the suffering or separate. If we both don't want that, we are going to have to work together." That's the key.

The space between the boundaries needs to be made safe. Who's going to work at it? Are you and your partner willing? Can you treat that between place as a kind of sacred space in which you both agree to act in the best interest of the relationship? And to make efforts to change directions if either of you falls down on the job? In other words, the third dimension has got to come alive. You've got to claim that space between the boundaries for emotional safety. Envision it as a place in which you can feel relaxed, accepted, thoughtful, considerate, loved, and loving. If you can see what you are aiming to create, you have a fighting chance at making it happen.

Love relationships need to be about love. For a slew of cultural and personal reasons, most of us do not know how, but need to learn how, to filter out elements that kill off the spirit of love between ourselves and our partners. Negotiating differences does not come naturally or easily to most. We come to relationships with too much fear and too little understanding of what genuine forgiveness entails. Many of us are confused about what emotional safety is. These are the necessary tools, and many of us show up to work on our relationships without them. We can't do the job unless we change that. And that change needs to be something we can practice every day.

What do we want in our relationships? For many of us, the goal is to sustain intimacy, friendship, and trust without those qualities being glued together out of desperation. We want to feel that we have chosen to be with our partners freely, and with freedom comes responsibility. When it comes to relationships, fulfilling responsibility involves awareness, mindfulness, compassion, and a method that incorporates building emotional safety. With this you'll have what you need to bring your relationship to its potential.

Appendix 1

Annotated List of Recommended Reading

Atkinson, Brent. *Emotional Intelligence in Couples Therapy*. New York: Norton. 2005.

An approach to couples work that is contemporary and interesting with numerous points of agreement with the three-dimensional method. Highly readable and recommended.

Benson, Herbert. *The Relaxation Response*. New York: Harper Collins. 1975.

A classic in the literature of meditation. This book provides an exercise for deep relaxation that is totally accessible and practicable.

*Burton, Richard A. *On Being Certain*. New York: St. Martin's Griffin. 2008.

A brilliant exposition on the nature of certainty as a psychological phenomenon. Good reading but not light reading.

Chabris, Christopher, and Simons, Daniel. *The Invisible Gorilla*. New York: Crown. 2010.

Readings in the psychology field do not get more entertaining than this. Chock full of fascinating studies and surprising perspectives, many of which pertain directly to interpersonal healing, although you've got to use your imagination to make the connections.

*Cozolino, Louis. *The Neuroscience of Pychotherapy*. New York: Norton. 2010.

This book is of great interest. Cozolino combines modern neuroscience with attachment theory. Recommended if you crave a readable book on fairly technical matters.

Damasio, Antonio. *Descartes' Error: Emotion, Reason, and the Brain.* New York: Penguin. 2005.

This is a fascinating read by a top neuroscientist. His perspective on emotion is part of the new wave that is changing the psychology field. Also highly readable.

Dweck, Carol S. *Mind-Set: The New Psychology of Success.* New York: Random House. 2005.

This book is a masterpiece of simplicity and power. It is a benchmark perspective that is both profound and completely down to earth.

Eagleman, David. *Incognito.* New York: Pantheon. 2011.

This neuroscientist focuses on the unreliability of memory and the biological bases for conditions that have been widely thought to be psychological. Written in a clear and accessible style. Recommended.

Hahn, Thich Nhat. *Anger.* New York: Riverhead/Penguin. 2001.

A classic. Wise and compassionate. Much grace and clarity.

Hanson, Rick, and Mendius, Richard. *Buddha's Brain.* Oakland: New Harbinger. 2009.

Very interesting and accessible. A best seller. Recommended.

*LeDoux, Joseph. *Synaptic Self.* New York: Penguin. 2003.

A highly technical book on neuroscience by a pioneer in the field. If you are interested in hard-core clinical neuroscience, this is recommended as a read or reference.

Newberg, Andrew, and Waldman, Mark. *Words Can Change Your Brian.* New York: Hudson Street. 2012.

Very useful, informative, accessible. Highly recommended.

*Ogden, Pat, and Minton, Kekuni, et al. *A Sensorimotor Approach to Psychotherapy.* New York: Norton. 2006.

A creative and highly influential approach to working with traumatic issues in psychotherapy. For those interested in understanding the sea-change in the field of psychotherapy, this book offers an interesting perspective. Written primarily for a professional audience.

*Panksepp, Jaak. *Affective Neuroscience.* New York: Oxford. 1998.

Highly technical. A good reference for those with a serious interest in learning about the brain.

Parker-Pope, Tara. *For Better: The Science of a Good Marriage.* New York: Dutton. 2010.

Some very useful information. You'll be surprised to learn about some of the research reported here. A good read.

*Porges, Stephen W. *The Polyvagal Theory.* New York: Norton. 1997.

A ground-breaking book. Highly technical. Not an easy read but for the person who wants to go to the source. Highly recommended. Interesting to note, despite the difficulty of the prose—highly academic and filled with jargon—you can learn about Porges through interviews and talks on YouTube.com. Whether interviewed or lecturing, the man is very accessible and a charming speaker and communicator.

Schwartz, Richard. *Internal Family Systems Therapy.* New York: Guildford, 1995.

This is another classic, though not writerly. It is a readable book that introduces a profound and humanistic therapy approach that is a genuine contribution to the field of psychotherapy. This book is not focused on couples work but the perspective of thinking about people, partners for example, in terms of the various well-developed parts that they present as important—similar in some ways to Panksepp's seven different emotional operating systems.

*Shapiro, Francine. *EMDR: Eye Movement Desensitization Reprocessing. Basic Principles, Protocols and Procedures.* Guildford: 2001.

Written primarily for professionals, this book provides a good overview for one of the most fascinating and innovative approaches to trauma available.

Siegel, Daniel J. *Mindsight.* New York: Bantam. 2011.

This author is another leading light in clinical neuroscience. This book is highly readable and interesting. A personal favorite.

Spring, Janis Abrahms. *After the Affair: Healing the Pain and Rebuilding Trust When a Partner Has Been Unfaithful.* New York: Harper Collins. 1996.

Another classic that therapists recommend to clients regularly. Empowering, useful, and wise.

Indicates that book is either somewhat or highly technical.

Appendix 2

Commentary on Empathy Awareness Responses

In terms of three-dimensional communication, I share my opinion about what it means if you have indicated that the situation described in the item reflects how your relationship is being conducted.

1) In the past two weeks I can recall at least one situation in which I gave my partner the benefit of a doubt.

   Figuring out what inhibits you from being able to do so is important. What does this say about the trust level in your relationship? Not feeling able to give your partner the benefit of the doubt is a red flag. Think about the history of this trend. Were you ever able to extend this trust? Do you feel that your partner gives you the benefit of the doubt? Being able to talk about this in a compassionate way might spark a move toward greater emotional safety.

2) I make a special effort to have my partner understand the ways in which I believe we see things eye to eye.

   Congratulations! This is the hallmark of an empathetic, compassionate, three-dimensional communication process. Validating the strengths of your relationship by explicitly stating them creates an atmosphere of trust and openness.

3) Even when my partner and I disagree, I rarely feel like I can't understand why he feels the way he does.

    That's impressive.

4) I would say that I am as interested in understanding my partner as I am in having my partner understand me.

    It sounds like your relationship has a lot going for it. Such a connection is precious.

5) When my partner and I disagree, I am curious to understand how and why she feels as she does.

    When partners share this attitude, the relationship has an excellent prognosis for success in the long term.

6) I criticize my partner too frequently.

    If you identify with this statement, you are acknowledging that you have an issue you need to work on. Your awareness of this is a good thing. Understanding how and why you feel the need to do this is important. Taking steps to do so will be important if you want to strengthen the communication process. Remember, talking about issues that bother you can be constructive if done with tact and compassion. Criticism implies a barrage, an attitude of disapproval that damages possibilities for connection. Use your awareness of the trend to stem it. It can be and often is a relationship destroyer.

7) When I criticize my partner, he usually takes it the wrong way.

    Most people respond negatively to criticism, so this should not be a surprise. When you say that your partner takes what you say the "wrong way," have you explained what the "right way," the way you wish to be understood, would be? If your intention when you criticize is to make things better, highlight your *intention*. And then find a different way to get across whatever you are trying to improve by offering this criticism. Use your partner's feedback about why he takes your criticism the "wrong way" to guide you toward getting your message across without offending or deflating him. Think about creating emotional safety.

8) I do not believe I do this, but my partner complains that I talk down to him.

> You do not believe you talk down to your partner but he says you do. Your attitude toward his complaint is of heightened importance. If you take his complaint seriously, you demonstrate an accepting attitude toward him rather than a contemptuous one. This affirms that you desire to connect and that you view his complaint as a problem you want to approach and solve together. This creates emotional safety.
>
> If you challenge his perception or in any way make light of his feelings, you miss an opportunity for healing. What is most important about this complaint is not whether it is correct but that it indicates disconnection. This is a time to get very curious and try to understand from his point of view how and why he feels this way. The goal here is to slow down the conversation so that each of you feels intimately familiar with the other's experience.

9) I don't mean to do it, but there are times I find myself talking down to my partner.

> If you identify with this statement, you obviously have been thinking about the relationship and are open to shouldering some responsibility for what needs to happen for the communication process to improve. This is an example of self-focus and can be the basis of effective change in relationships. The next step, actually changing your behavior and refraining from talking down to your partner, is not easy but certainly can be done. Here are some techniques that can be helpful: keep a journal. In it jot down instances when you speak to your partner in ways that you feel are not productive. Note the circumstances under which this occurs. Think about whether a pattern emerges. Talk to your partner about it and let her know that you do not feel good about talking down to her. Enlist her help in your effort to become as aware as you can be of the pattern you are trying to change. Explicitly acknowledge the problem you have identified with your partner. This will likely increase trust between you and your partner. Persist in your efforts. Change like this takes consistency and resolve.

10) When I argue with my partner, most of the time I find myself waiting for him to finish talking so I can make my point.

   It sounds like you get preoccupied with what you want to say and stop listening to your partner when you argue. Maybe talking about what is going on while you are listening would help both of you to connect. As it is, there seems to be no dialogue, no back-and-forth. Are you waiting for him to finish, which indicates you are not listening closely, because you have given up on learning anything new about how your partner feels? Do you feel that your partner repeats what he says and is predictable in what he is saying? Ordinarily, when partners repeat a statement, there is a good chance they feel unheard. Have you clearly indicated and validated that you have gotten his message? When you say you are waiting to make your point, it seems clear that you are not concerned with acknowledging or appreciating your partner's point. It sounds like you argue debate-style, that the conversations have a competitive edge. Where is the third dimension?

   Consider these ideas: Are you too angry to listen? Are you contemptuous of your partner's perspective? Is it difficult for you to engage your curiosity about how he is thinking? Feeling that you know what he is about to say is often a tip-off that you are taking a combative, oppositional stance. Go back to thinking about creating emotional safety. Do not debate your partner on the content of what he says but on whether his remark brings you closer together or pushes you away. And when you do that, make it clear that you do not want to open up the distance between you, unless of course you do. If you do, it sounds like what you are doing now will bring that about.

11) Patience is something I've developed and learned to help me create understandings.

   That is a huge achievement. Congratulations!

12) I want my partner to understand me. That is to say, I'd like her to be familiar not only with what my opinions are but with the way I've come to the opinions that I have.

This is an excellent sign. This is a hallmark of a three-dimensional communication process, the basis of intimate sharing that leads to knowing and being known by your partner.

13) When my partner tells me how he feels about something, I do not ask how he came to feel the way he does. I feel that understanding him on that level is almost an invasion of his privacy.

     Although respect for privacy is important, I would urge you to test the waters and ask enough questions to find out how much your partner would like to share with you. Don't make assumptions without exploring the issue in conversation. Not asking pertinent questions can be understood as a lack of interest in him rather than as respect for privacy. Sometimes your partner may need encouragement to share additional information that he would like you to know; that is by no means unusual. On the other hand, many partners share what they wish to and appreciate not feeling any pressure to go further. So it pays to ask in a tactful way.

14) I recall when I first understood that my partner's political leanings differed from my own in significant ways. I wondered whether this would create an insurmountable problem for us.

     This is a fair question, and differences in perspective and values can create difficulties. Your posing this as a question indicates to me that you wish to explore the issue in an open manner. Generally speaking, some couples have carved out good relationships even though they hold dramatically different political views. The key is whether you both can maintain mutual respect for the differences. Even if you had identical values and political opinions, if your conversation about the similarities were not respectful of the manner in which each of you voiced your shared perspective, the upshot could be disconnection. In a nutshell, I wouldn't emphasize the differences in opinion but the emotional quality of the dialogue you have about those differences.

15) My partner has a very different relationship with his family of origin than I do. I recognize that I can't change his relationship with his parents, but often wish that I could.

The key here is that you recognize that you can't change his relationship with his parents. Use that as a standard to help your not go off on a tangent. Unless he asks you for specific help with his parents, do not take on the thankless task of offering help that has not been requested. What is generally helpful in situations like this is for you to convey feelings of empathy with his position vis-à-vis his parents. For example, if he has a hard time when he visits his parents, you can let him know that you understand how difficult it is for him. You can also offer to be of any help that he feels he might be able to use, assuming you feel that way. However, taking the initiative to try to change the long-standing relationship between him and his family would be an exercise in futility and could likely create resentment in the long run.

Appendix 3

Gina and Tim Follow-Up

Unfortunately, by the time Gina and Tim came to me, Tim was unable to open to the possibility that they could make the changes he felt he needed. He acknowledged that he had run short of patience, and, although he was furious about the pattern of lying and spying—the cell phone was only one dimension of it—he still felt affection for Gina and departed from the relationship with sadness and humility. He expressed regret that there was nothing that would make him feel hopeful that he could trust her again.

Gina was sad and tried to remotivate him with promises, but in the end he was not receptive. However, it seemed that based on his responses and the lack of evidence that he had been anything but a faithful and caring partner, she felt a loss. But at the same time, she came to a realization that "Tim might have been a good partner for me if we'd met at a different time in my life, but, for whatever reasons, I wasn't ready for whatever we could have had at this time in my life." In any case, it seemed that she was feeling the bud of hopefulness that at some point she could be more trusting and develop a different, less defensive, and fearful position in relation to a partner. Although she hadn't achieved what she might have wanted to with Tim, she felt that she herself had learned some important things about herself, not all of which were flattering.

The couples therapy was brief, but Gina stayed on for a course of individual sessions. The reasons she felt fearful of taking a chance on trusting Tim had been invisible to her. She was able to allow herself to get in touch with feelings that she intuited were there only because she felt that *something* was bothering her, *something* was making her feel uneasy and unsettled, but she had been more invested in avoiding that *something* than opening herself to the possibility of understanding how it fit into the way she thought and felt about herself. Once these shadowy forces became more familiar to her, feelings of rejection and self-doubt that preceded her unfortunate love affairs prior to meeting Tim tapered off. She seemed to become less involved with the *feeling* that the entire issue of being blindsided was a kind of fate she was destined to experience. Perhaps her greatest fear was not that she would be betrayed by the men in her life but that she would not allow herself to feel free enough to attempt to build a relationship that could be satisfying. She began to trust that she would not blindside herself with lapses of confidence in her ability to love and be loved. She began to think that she would be able to stave off negative thinking about what the future would bring long enough to develop some positive images—plans, hopes, and dreams—that she could bring with her into new relationships. She continued working with me for some time and made appreciable progress in her next relationship. The obsessively jealous focus no longer remained central for her, and she was appreciably more relaxed and secure in her feeling of connection to her next partner.

Appendix 4

Response to Exercise in Chapter Four

On the surface, I would say that Carole missed an opportunity to connect with Jim when, instead of affirming her basic agreement with what he said, she criticized him for what he has failed to do in relation to the statement he made. However, in her defense, it can be said that in introducing herself to me, she wanted it to be known that she was not simply interested in having a conversation in which she and Jim sounded like they knew how to get along. She wanted to cut to the nitty-gritty and let me know that there was more going on than his statement would imply on its surface. On the other hand, perhaps Jim had not been living up to the statement that he made. A vote of confidence in his ability to at least see the problem clearly, whether or not he was able to act on it directly, might have brought him the support he needed to do better. In other words, because he hadn't yet *walked the walk*, that doesn't prove he doesn't want to or can't develop the ability to do just that. For many, *talking the talk* is the preliminary step and eventually leads to being able to walk that way as well. So the subject is complicated. There are times when confrontational response shuts down a partner, as Carole's did, and times when it alerts a partner to seeing things in a way that hadn't occurred to them.

Appendix 5

If Abuse Is The Issue

This book is designed to help couples deal with dysfunctional communication. However, if you believe that your relationship involves a form of abuse, you do not need a long-range plan that will improve the way you and your partner communicate but instead a means to escape harm.

If you are in a crisis in which your physical safety is imperiled, the techniques in this book will not be helpful to you now, not until you remove yourself from harm's way.

If you consider your relationship abusive but fail to respond to it as if it were in crisis, you may well be enabling the abuse. If you believe this may be the case, I would advise you to contact a licensed therapist in your area immediately.

Response to abuse requires action. Once you've secured your safety, it may be possible to think about implementing a three-dimensional solution with your partner if he has received treatment himself or begun his recovery in earnest or both.

If you need help immediately, call 911.

Other sources of help:

National Domestic Violence Hot Line: 1-800-799-7233
Drug and Alcohol Abuse Services: 1-800-784-6776

Appendix 6

EXPLORING THREE DIMENSIONS
Response to Exercise 1.1

GEORGE AND MARIE

First Dimension: George's words convey a clear message of frustration. Christine's response indicates she understands what he is saying on a literal level. The problem in communication here does not exist in the first dimension.

Second Dimension: The emotional subtext of George's message radiates with frustration, which is coherent with the words he speaks. Christine's mocks him, demonstrating defensiveness. She fends off, rather than takes in, his message.

Third Dimension: George tries to create emotional safety by calling attention to a problem in the relationship that he feels needs work. Christine shows no evidence here of safeguarding their connection. She counterattacks. She neither acknowledges nor seems to appreciate that he is trying to connect with her. There is no clear sign that she takes his concerns seriously. Their third dimension is not functional and they are therefore vulnerable to furthering disconnection between them.

VALERIE AND CHARLOTTE

First Dimension: Both partners stay with one another's message. They locate and connect to one another with their statements.

Second Dimension: Although they start out with a difference in what they would like to see happen in terms of money management, each is accepting of the other's concerns. The second dimension here contains openness, and willingness to engage and extend.

Third Dimension: This couple is able to achieve a three-dimensional understanding. They are able to demonstrate enough internal flexibility to grasp each other's viewpoint. They get through talking about a difference without resorting to blame or reproach at any time. The third dimension is nicely developed here.

COURTNEY AND CHRIS

First Dimension: This couple clearly communicates what is on their minds. No problem in the first dimension.

Second Dimension: They position themselves as willing to see things from one another's point of view. They validate one another's perspective and express appreciation for each other's contributions to the dialogue. Willingness to connect and generosity are elements in their dialogue.

Third Dimension: They make clear to one another that when they communicate about a stressful issue, it helps them both feel good about one another. This is a good example of a couple creating emotional safety together.

Response to Exercise 1.2

ALANA AND KEITH

First Dimension: Alana requests a favor of Keith but, at first, fails to spell out what the favor entails. He consents to deliver the favor without being clear about what he is being asked to do. This is miscommunication in the first dimension.

Second Dimension: Alana's underlying emotion in this talk appears to be apprehension and anxiety. Keith's appears to be a brusque defensiveness and bristling impatience.

Third Dimension: The issue of Keith's drinking seems to be heightened prior to this conversation. Having to work it out in the moment, with the issue of driving safety adding to the pressure, makes it all the more difficult for either partner to respond compassionately. Yet, we sometimes have to meet these kinds of pressures head on and have limited time to work through them. In this case, physical safety may be an issue, and they are forced, by circumstance, to press difficult issues. Alana asks for what she needs and that is a positive contribution to the dialogue and can be thought of as a means to create safety, emotional and physical in this case. Keith responds defensively. There is no sign that he sees her request from her point of view. His irritation comes on immediately, and he responds on automatic pilot, without reflection. At this point, the third dimension in their dialogue appears to be dysfunctional. This hot button issue will require much time and dialogue, and their attention to it will be a test of their commitment to the relationship.